DECEMBER

Make the Most of Every Month with Carson-Dellosa's Monthly Books!

Production Manager
Chris McIntyre

Editorial Director
Jennifer Weaver-Spencer

Writers
Lynette Pyne
Amy Gamble
Joan Daniels
L. Marie Lavallee
Linda Ludlow
Joan Shortle
Sara Sightes
Trisha Yates

Editors
Maria McKinney
Kelly Gunzenhauser
Carol Layton

Art Directors
Penny Casto
Alain Barsony

Art Coordinator
Edward Fields

Illustrators
Mike Duggins
Erik Huffine
David Lackey
Ray Lambert
Bill Neville
Betsy Peninger
J.J. Rudisill
Pam Thayer
Todd Tyson
Julie Webb

Cover Design
Amber Kocher Crouch
Ray Lambert
J.J. Rudisill

D1611279

Carson-Dellosa Publishing Company, Inc.

DECEMBER

Table of Contents

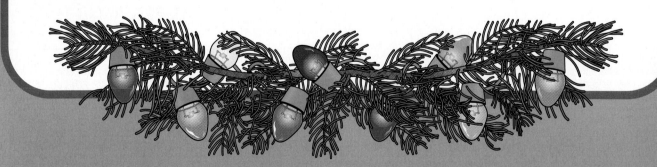

DECEMBER TEACHER TIPS

Letters Made Easy
Put up bulletin board letters straight the first time using a length of yarn as a guide. Use a ruler and a pencil to mark a beginning and an ending point on the board. Secure a length of yarn across the board by placing a push pin through both marks. Line up the letters above the yarn to ensure they are straight. Remove the yarn when complete.

Choose a Helper
Make choosing classroom helpers fair and easy. Provide two empty juice containers. Then, write each student's name on a wooden craft stick and place them in a container. Choose a stick and allow the student whose name appears on it to be the helper. As students are chosen, place their name sticks in the empty container to ensure everyone will have a chance to help.

Holiday Greetings
Use simple holiday patterns to create classroom greeting cards. Cut out several seasonal shapes from colorful paper and add your holiday greetings. Tape a candy cane or other holiday treat to the shape and give them to students.

Supply Boxes
As the holidays approach and you begin to complete more craft activities, set up supply boxes to save time. Place enough crayons, glue, scissors, and other supplies in a shoe box for each table of students. Designate one student from each table to distribute and collect supplies.

Festive Borders
Double the life of your bulletin board border strips by allowing students to draw holiday or theme-related artwork on the blank side of commercial border strips. Display the borders to add a personal touch to classroom displays.

Special Memories
As a special gift to parents, tape-record an interview with each student. Ask questions, such as "What is your favorite thing about school?" If desired, have students sing a holiday song and send a holiday greeting. Provide stickers and markers for students to decorate their tapes, then let them give the tapes to their parents as gifts.

December

Day-by-Day Calendar

1 *Cookie Cutter Week* is December 1-7. Have students bring in different shaped cookie cutters and bake a batch of cookies.

2 *Georges Seurat's Birthday* The French artist and inventor of pointillism was born in 1859. Have students create a picture made of different colored dots. Lightly sketch drawings with a pencil. Then, make dots with crayons or markers to fill in the color.

3 *Aardvark Week* is the first week in December. Have students write and illustrate acrostic poems about aardvarks.

4 *Bingo Month* Celebrate with a game of bingo.

5 *Walt Disney's Birthday* The motion picture producer was born in 1901. Have students write a dialog between themselves and their favorite Disney characters.

6 The *Republic of Mexico* was *established* on this day in 1822. Have a piñata party with the class.

7 *Delaware became the first state* on this day in 1787. Have students locate Delaware on a map and name its capital.

8 The *first greeting card* was *printed* on this day in 1843. Have students create greeting cards for friends or family members.

9 *Jean de Brunhoff's Birthday* The creator of Babar was born on this day in 1899. Have students choose an animal and write an adventure story about it.

10 *The Nobel Prize ceremonies* are *held* today. There are awards for physics, chemistry, physiology and medicine, literature, economics, and peace. The winners receive money, a medal, and a diploma. Have students design a medal for the Nobel Prize in a school subject of their choice.

11 *UNICEF* was *established* on this day in 1946. UNICEF helps children all over the world get food and other items. Have students create posters encouraging people to help others during the holidays.

12 *Tell Someone They're Doing a Good Job Week* is December 12-18. Have students write a letter to a person of their choice thanking them for the good job they are doing.

13 *International Calendar Awareness Month* Divide students into groups of two or three. Assign each group a month of the year. Have each group create a picture to represent that month. Combine the pictures into a class calendar.

14 *Nostradamus's Birthday* Born in 1503, he predicted many important world events. Have students make predictions about January. Save the predictions and open them next month.

15 *Alexandre Gustave Eiffel's Birthday* The French engineer was born in 1832. Compare his Eiffel Tower to other large buildings such as the Sears Tower and the Empire State Building.

16 *Ludwig Van Beethoven's Birthday* The composer was born in 1770. Have students listen to some of his music and paint a picture to show how the music effects them.

17 *Wilbur and Orville Wright made the first powered airplane flight* today in 1903. Make paper airplanes. See whose flies the farthest.

18 *The Thirteenth Amendment* was *ratified* in 1865 outlawing slavery. Write freedom slogans and decorate them with symbols of peace.

19 *Poor Richard's Almanac* was *first published* on this day in 1732. Write almanac scavenger hunt questions on index cards to pass to students. Have them look in *Poor Richard's Almanac* to find the answers.

20 *International Language Week* is the third week in December. Put foreign language dictionaries in the classroom. Write five words on the board and have students find the words in each language by the end of the day.

21 *The first crossword puzzle appeared* in an American newspaper today in 1913. Let each student create a crossword puzzle and then switch with a friend.

22 *The thermometer* was *invented* on this day in 1593 by Galileo. Measure and record the temperature inside and outside.

23 *Metric Conversion Act Anniversary* Have students measure and weigh different objects in the class in standard and metric units.

24 *Silent Night* was *composed* today in 1818. Have students write a new holiday song using a familiar tune.

25 *Isaac Newton's Birthday* Born in 1642, he discovered that objects fall at the same rate regardless of their mass. Have students drop two objects, one heavier than the other, and see which lands first.

26 *Read a New Book Month* Have students read a book and present a book report to the class.

27 *Louis Pasteur's Birthday* Born in 1822, he made milk safe to drink with the invention of pasteurization. Have students make a collage of products that are safe to eat and drink thanks to Pasteur.

28 *Chewing Gum* was *patented* on this day in 1869. Have students design wrappers for a new bubble gum. Wrap the papers around pieces of foil and display on a bulletin board.

29 *National Stress-Free Family Holidays Month* Have students brainstorm a list of how they can help make the holidays stress-free.

30 *Rudyard Kipling's Birthday* The author of *The Jungle Book* and *Just So Stories* was born in 1865. Read a *Just So* story. Then, have students write one of their own.

31 *New Year's Eve* Have students share good memories of the past year with the class.

5

December

Sunday	Monday	Tuesday	Wednesday	Thursday	Friday	Saturday

December Gazette

Teacher _____   Date _____

IN THE NEWS

WHAT'S COMING UP

TAKE NOTE

KID'S CORNER

2●   1★   ●19
3●   ●18
4●   ●17
5●   ●16
6●   ●15
7●   ●14
8●   ●13
9●   10●   11●   12●

Celebrate December!

Dear Family Members,
Here are a few quick-and-easy activities to help you and your child celebrate special days throughout the month of December.

Hanukkah **is an eight-day celebration in the Jewish faith, also known as** *The Festival of Lights*
- The observance begins on the twenty-fifth day of the Hebrew month of Kislev, which falls in November or December. Dreidel is a popular game that is played during Hanukkah celebrations. Purchase a dreidel and play the game as a family.

Kwanzaa **is celebrated during December**
- Kwanzaa is a nonreligious holiday celebrated each year from December 26th until January 1st. The word Kwanzaa means *first fruits* in Kiswahili. The holiday was created in 1966 by Maulana Karenga as a way for people to celebrate African traditions and culture. The customs and symbols of Kwanzaa come from African harvest festivals. Handmade gifts called zwardi (zah•WAH•dee) are given during Kwanzaa. Draw family names and help your child make a gift to give to the family member selected.

The first greeting card was printed **on December 8, 1843**
- Work with your child to make holiday greeting cards using markers and stickers. Send the cards to family friends and relatives.

Poinsettia Day **is on December 12**
- Dr. Joel Roberts Poinsett introduced this Mexican plant to the U.S. in 1828. Let your child pick out a poinsettia plant to enjoy during the holidays. Let your child also choose a place to put the plant in the house and be responsible for watering it. (Poinsettias are poisonous to cats and dogs.)

Christmas **is on December 25**
Work with your child to make a glowing Christmas tree ornament using green construction paper, colored tissue paper, and glue. For each ornament, have your child cut out two Christmas tree shapes from green paper. Use a hole punch to punch holes in one of the trees. Glue squares of colored tissue paper over the holes. Glue the second tree pattern to the back of the first to cover the tissue paper. Make a hanger by attaching a yarn or string loop to the top of the ornament.

New Year's Eve **is December 31**
- Let your child make a New Year's party hat. Cut a half-circle from paper and roll it into a cone shape. Staple or tape the hat to fit your child's head. Have her decorate the hat using markers, colored paper, and glue.

Read In December!

Dear Family Members,
Here are some books to share with your child to enhance the enjoyment of reading in December.

 The Twelve Days of Christmas by Jan Brett
- *The detailed artwork complements the rhythmic reading of the classic English carol.*
- Have your child make a personalized version of the twelve days of Christmas by naming what he or she would like to receive on each of the twelve days.

 The Family Christmas Tree Book by Tomie DePaola
- *A family talks about the origin and history of the Christmas tree as they decorate their own tree.*
- Provide colored paper, crayons, and glue for your child to use to make his or her own Christmas tree ornament.

 Joy to the World by Savior Pirotta
- *Features five folk tales about Christmas celebrations around the world.*
- Ask your child to think of things that are similar between his or her family's holiday traditions and those from the book.

 The Polar Express by Chris Van Allsburg
- *One Christmas Eve, a boy takes a magical journey to the North Pole on a train called* The Polar Express.
- Line up several chairs and pretend you and your child are riding on the Polar Express. Describe what you see as you sip warm cocoa.

 Hanukkah Lights, Hanukkah Nights by Leslie Kimmelman
- *An entire family enjoys the traditions and customs of Hanukkah together.*
- While looking through the book, have your child name some Hanukkah words.

 Inside-Out Grandma by Joan Rothenberg
- *Grandma explains her unusual way of remembering to buy enough oil to make potato latkes for the Hanukkah celebration.*
- Work with your child to make potato latkes using the recipe at the end of the book.

 My First Kwanzaa Book by Deborah M. Newton Chocolate
- *Introduces children to the history, symbols, and meaning of the Kwanzaa celebration.*
- Provide construction paper, markers, glue, and wooden craft sticks. Help your child make a kinara by coloring and gluing the sticks to the paper.

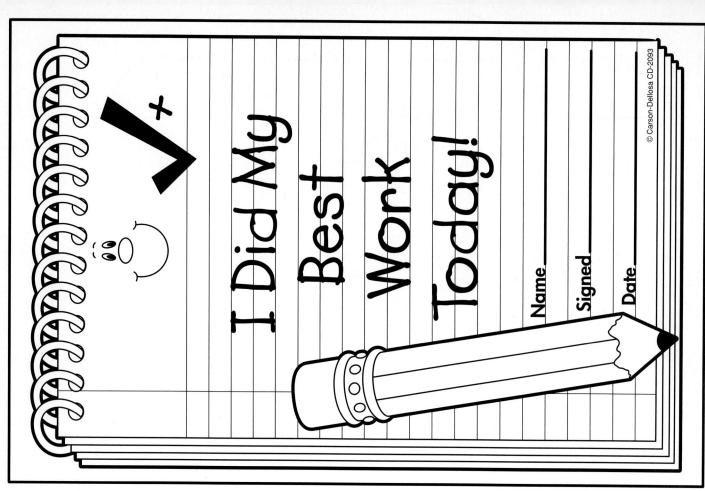

✓+

I Did My Best Work Today!

Name _____
Signed _____
Date _____

YOU REALLY SHINE!

_____ IS A STAR STUDENT!

Signed _____
Date _____

10

No Homework Tonight!

Name _____

Signed _____

Date _____

Sweet Work!

To _____

For _____

Signed _____

Date _____

DECEMBER
Writing Activities

Offer students a way to express excitement about the holidays by writing about the month's special events. December writing activities can be used in holiday cards, artwork projects, or given as gifts!

Word Bank Words

holiday	holly	presents
celebrate	candle	wreath
tradition	lights	pinecone
custom	gingerbread	star
evergreen	peppermint	poinsettia

Spelling Match

Pass out index cards to students. Have pairs of students write the same spelling word on their cards so that you will have two of each spelling word. Have small groups use the cards to play a matching game. Turn all of the cards face down on a table. Each player chooses two cards and turns them over. If the words match, the player takes the cards and gets another turn. If the cards do not match, the next player takes a turn. Have the players read and spell the words on the cards they choose. Play continues until all the cards have been matched.

holiday
holiday

Three Wishes

Wish I may, wish I might...Have students imagine they have been granted three wishes for the holiday season. Have them write about what they would wish for and why.

Home Sweet Gumdrop

Let students draw sweet treats! Show children pictures of gingerbread houses, then have students draw the houses, and write descriptions using their senses. Direct students to describe how the houses look, smell, feel, and taste. Let students read their descriptions to partners and let the partners draw the houses based on their descriptions. When the drawings are complete, have students and partners compare their drawings.

My house smells delicious, like a cake that just came out of the oven. It is covered in colorful candies of all shapes and sizes. Four huge candy canes hold up the frosting covered roof.

Giving Gifts

December is the season for giving! Give each child a piece of paper to decorate as wrapping paper. On the inside, have each child write about a gift she gave someone, explaining why she chose the gift and the person's reaction when he received it. Fold the papers into package shapes and place them in a basket for students to enjoy during free time.

Thank You

Thanks a bunch! Have each student write a friendly thank-you letter for a gift she has received. Have students format their letters with appropriate greetings, closings, and dates. Allow students to mail or hand deliver their thank-you letters.

Wintertime Inventions

Have students make their lives easier! Ask each student to invent a product that would be useful in the winter or for the December holidays, such as *Know-it-Now Glasses* (eyeglasses that can see through wrapping paper) or *Super Freeze Snowman Spray* (makes snowmen last through summer). Ask children to think about their own recent activities and any obstacles they have encountered. Would a new invention have helped? Have students write and illustrate newspaper advertisements for their new inventions. Post the ads on a bulletin board covered with the classified pages of a newspaper. Title the display *Young Inventors!*

Editing Folders

Set up an editing station where children can leave work to be proofread and proofread other students' work. Label a folder *To be Proofread* and another *To be Returned*. When a student places a paper in the *To be Proofread* folder, have him remove a classmate's paper to check and place in the *To be Returned* folder.

Winter Haiku

Students can celebrate a favorite winter activity or occurrence by writing a haiku poem about it. Haiku are unrhymed poems of three lines containing five, seven, and five syllables, respectively. They are usually light and delicate in feeling and explore the beauty of nature or the season of the year.
For example:

Snowflakes are falling
Softly and gently they come
Covering the grass.

Bulletin Board Ideas

Let students find winter homes for animals with this interactive bulletin board. Create a winter scene by covering a bulletin board with white paper. Add two trees made from brown paper and a pond made from blue paper. Copy ten animal patterns (pages 48-51) and create ten animal homes around the board as follows: bear and fox = cave, groundhog and chipmunk = burrow, frog = mud in pond, raccoon and mouse = tree hollow, skunk = log, deer and rabbit = pile of leaves and twigs under tree. Put a hook and loop tape dot on the back of each animal and on each home. Place the animals in an envelope stapled to the bulletin board and let students match the animals to their correct winter homes. This display makes a great interactive activity to use with the *Animals in Winter* chapter (pages 36-51).

Students will make tracks toward good work with this bulletin board. Cover a bulletin board with blue paper. Cut out animal tracks from sandpaper and black construction paper, using page 46 as a reference. Use the black tracks as a border for the display. Glue the sandpaper tracks to index cards and label with the appropriate animal name. Students can place paper over the sandpaper tracks and rub with crayons. Cut out the tracks and label each with a student name and an animal name. Accent excellent winter work with the tracks. Display this bulletin board during the *Animals in Winter* chapter (pages 36-51).

14

Help students think of others at the holidays by writing about a gift they wish they could give the world. Cut wrapping paper to match the size of writing paper and staple it along the top of the paper. Decorate the wrapping paper and cover with ribbon to resemble a present. Have students write paragraphs about their gifts on the writing paper. Place a large Earth in the center of the bulletin board. Display the "gifts" on the outer edge of the Earth and add a border of bows. Title the bulletin board *Our Gifts to the World*. This display coordinates well with the *Christmas Throughout the World* chapter (pages 52-72).

Use the reference in the *Christmas Throughout the World* chapter (pages 54-67) to write a list of holiday greetings from various countries. Let children make Christmas cards and write different countries' greetings on each card. Display the cards on the bulletin board in a big mailbox, cut from butcher paper, with the cards spilling out. Attach envelopes with different country names and challenge students to put each card in its correct envelope. You may wish to display this bulletin board during the *Christmas Throughout the World* chapter (pages 52-72).

15

Your students will love decorating Christmas trees from around the world with this bulletin board idea. Enlarge and cut out five evergreen tree patterns (page 77) from green butcher paper. For the Italian tree, cut a brown triangle the same size as the trees to represent a ceppo. Separate students into six groups and let each group decorate a tree from a different country. Use the information provided in the *Christmas Throughout the World* chapter (pages 54-67) and Christmas books as reference. When completed, display the trees on a bulletin board and have each group label its tree with the country's name, flag, and holiday greeting. Examples of countries with their tree decorations are: Mexico: lights, paper flowers, pottery; Germany: candles, apples, spice cookies; France: foil stars, fruit, lights, pine cones; England: candles, cornucopias, fruits; Italy: triangular ladder decorated with candles, ornaments, small gifts, family treasures, nativity scenes. This display complements the *Christmas Throughout the World* (pages 52-72) chapter.

Give students a reason to celebrate! Cover a bulletin board with yellow paper and decorate it like a place mat. Use construction paper cut into fringe to create a border. Write the names of the symbols and fruits of Kwanzaa on slips of paper. Have each child choose a paper, then illustrate and cut out the chosen symbol. The *Kwanzaa* chapter patterns (pages 86-88) can be used for reference. Post the finished student work to create a cooperative Kwanzaa display. Use this bulletin board while you study the *Kwanzaa* chapter (pages 78-88).

16

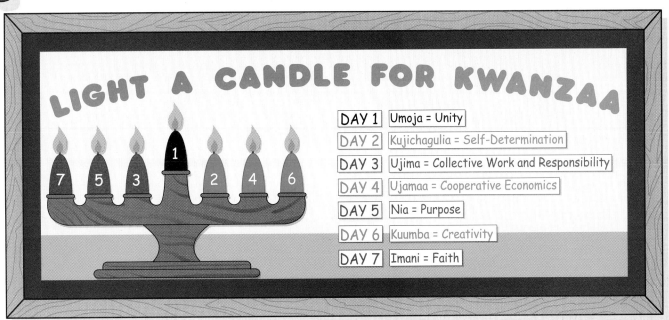

LIGHT A CANDLE FOR KWANZAA

DAY 1	Umoja = Unity
DAY 2	Kujichagulia = Self-Determination
DAY 3	Ujima = Collective Work and Responsibility
DAY 4	Ujamaa = Cooperative Economics
DAY 5	Nia = Purpose
DAY 6	Kuumba = Creativity
DAY 7	Imani = Faith

Here's a bulletin board that will help students remember the principles of Kwanzaa. Enlarge the kinara pattern (page 87). Trace the kinara onto self-adhesive paper with a wood grain pattern and cut out. Adhere the kinara to the bulletin board. Cut candle shapes from green, red, and black construction paper and top each with a yellow paper flames. Write the numbers shown above on the correct candles, then write the days and principles on strips of paper and hang them to the side of the kinara: *unity, self-determination, collective work and responsibility, cooperative economics, purpose, creativity,* and *faith.* Refer to the display as you study the *Kwanzaa* chapter (pages 78-88).

COOL READING

Get students in the mood for reading. Cover a bulletin board with blue paper. Share several books with the class that have wintertime themes. Have students choose a favorite book to describe. Students can create book jackets for their chosen books by cutting jacket shapes from two pieces of construction paper. Attach the two jacket shapes and let students decorate the top jacket. Then, cut down the center of the top jacket. Have students attach their book reports to the insides of their covers. Accent the display with icicles cut from aluminum foil attached to the edges of the board. This display complements the *A Wonderland of Winter Books* chapter (pages 89-92).

17

SLIDING INTO WINTER FUN

Slide into wintertime fun with this festive display. Cover a bulletin board with blue paper and use white paper to create snow slopes. Have students decorate two copies of the gingerbread man pattern (page 24) and two copies of the candy cane pattern (page 24) identically. Then, have students use the candy canes to create sleds for the gingerbread cutouts. Tack the gingerbread men and the candy canes on a bulletin board. Let students try to match each pair. This display works well with the *Gingerbread and Peppermint* unit (pages 20-25).

Spotlight sweet work with this bulletin board. Have each student cut out a candy cane pattern (page 24) and use a red marker to write his name into the stripes of the pattern. Then, have students color the candy canes any color they choose. Use these unique candy canes to accent exceptional student work. You may want to use this display with the *Gingerbread and Peppermint* chapter (pages 20-25).

18

Use this bulletin board to greet students each day during Hanukkah. Title the display *Happy Hanukkah.* Enlarge the Star of David pattern (page 33) onto yellow paper. Cut out the inside portions of the star so that the bulletin board background shows through, and display it in the upper left corner of the board. Copy the dreidel and menorah patterns (pages 33) and have students color them. Decorate the patterns using glitter and sequins, if desired. Add gold foil or paper gelt. Display the symbols on the bulletin board during the *Hanukkah* chapter (pages 26-35).

Leave students spinning with excitement when you display this bulletin board. Enlarge the dreidel pattern (page 33) and decorate it. Place the decorated dreidel pattern on the left side of the bulletin board. Have each student draw a circle on gold wrapping paper and cut out to resemble gelt. Use several dreidel patterns as a border. Display each student's best work, along with her gold gelt, on the bulletin board. Use this display with the *Hanukkah* chapter (pages 26-35).

Gingerbread and Peppermint

Gingerbread men and candy canes bring to mind the festivities and delights of the holiday season. Use these craft, writing, and game ideas to add some sugar and spice to your holiday lessons.

Did You Know?

- The gingerbread man story originates from a tale about Johnny Boys, which are human-shaped figures made from bread dough. One day while a Johnny Boy was baking in the oven, springy dough caused him to pop out of the oven and "escape." As gingerbread cookies became more popular, the tale of the Gingerbread Boy emerged.
- Today's gingerbread houses were inspired by the candy and cake house in the tale *Hansel and Gretel*.
- A choirmaster in Germany bent sugar sticks into the shape of shepherds' staffs and gave them to children in the congregation. These treats later became known as candy canes.

Literature Selections

Listed below are several versions of the Gingerbread Man story.

The Gingerbread Man by Eric A. Kimmel: Holiday House, 1993. (Picture book, 32 pg.)

The Gingerbread Boy by Paul Galdone: Clarion Books, 1975. (Picture book, 32 pg.)

The Legend of the Candy Cane by Lori Walburg: Zondervan Publishing House, 1997. (Picture book, 32 pg.) When a candymaker moves to a small town, he shares the story of the candy cane with its children.

Gingerbread and Peppermint Garland

Add a sweet touch to your classroom with gingerbread and peppermint garlands. Let students trace gingerbread man patterns (page 24) onto oaktag or poster board and cut them out. Decorate the cutouts using paints, markers, buttons, yarn, and small candies. Tape the end of a candy cane behind each gingerbread man's hand and connect the gingerbread men by interlocking the candy cane hooks. Reinforce the garland by taping the gingerbread men to a length of yarn. Use the garland to accent bulletin board displays, hallways, or doors.

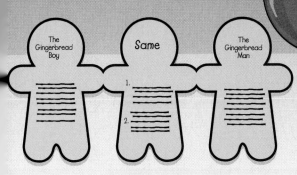

A Batch of Gingerbread Stories

The story of the gingerbread man is centuries old, which may explain why many different versions exist. After reading two versions of the story (see literature selections, page 20), have students make comparisons between the characters, settings, and plots using Venn diagrams. Accordion fold a 9" x 12" piece of construction paper in thirds. Trace the gingerbread man pattern (page 24) with the hands and feet on the folds, and cut out the patterns so that they are joined like paper dolls. Write the titles of the stories being compared on the tops of the left and right patterns. Below the titles, write the differences between the stories. In the center pattern, write the similarities. When everyone has made their Venn diagram, use the information to make a class list of comparisons.

His Side of the Story

Most people know how the gingerbread man sprang from the oven, escaped the kitchen, and teased the animals, but has anyone ever heard his version of the story? On gingerbread men patterns (page 24), instruct students to write stories explaining the famous tale from the gingerbread man's point of view . When the stories are complete, cut two 9" x 9" construction paper squares and decorate one to look like an oven. Make an oven "window" by cutting out the center of the square and gluing plastic wrap over the opening. Wrap and glue aluminum foil around the second square of paper to resemble a cookie sheet. Fan fold a strip of construction paper and glue one end to the foil-covered paper and the other to the back of the gingerbread man. Staple the bottom edge of the oven over the foil-covered square, so when the oven is opened, the gingerbread man "leaps out."

Gingerbread Picture Frames

Frame your students' pictures with specially made gingerbread houses. Copy one gingerbread house frame and roof pattern (page 25) for each student. Instruct students to trace two gingerbread house patterns onto brown craft foam or poster board and one roof pattern onto white craft foam or poster board. Cut out all of the pieces. Assist students in cutting a circle for a small photograph in the center of one house pattern. Glue the photograph between the house patterns, centering it in the opening. Glue the edges of the patterns closed. Glue the roof to the top of the house. Using sequins, pieces of pipe cleaner, and construction paper, decorate the gingerbread house. Attach magnetic tape to the back of the frame for display on a refrigerator. Let students take the frames home to give as holiday gifts.

Scratch and Sniff Gingerbread Men

These sweet-smelling gingerbread men will make delightful classroom displays. Have each child trace the gingerbread man pattern (page 24) on the back of medium-grade sandpaper. Cut out the patterns. Add a holiday scent by rubbing a cinnamon stick or peppermint oil across the sandpaper. Use white puffy paint to add faces and details. When dry, punch a hole in the top of the decoration, thread ribbon through the hole, and tie the ends together to create a hanger.

Peppermint Swirl Ornaments

Peppermint candies add a festive touch to gingerbread houses and holiday decorations alike. Let each child cut a 6" circle from poster board and color red or green swirls on both sides so it resembles a peppermint candy. Wrap a piece of clear cellophane around the candy, twist the ends, and secure with clear tape. Add several drops of peppermint extract for a "scent"sational touch.

Candy Cane Stripes

Let students be "candy stripers" for a day! Trace the candy cane pattern (page 24) onto white poster board or heavy construction paper. Provide pinking shears for students to cut out the shapes. Create stripes on the candy cane pattern by taping one end of a length of red yarn to the back of the design and wrapping the yarn around the candy cane. Secure the end of the yarn with tape. Punch a hole in the top of the decoration, thread ribbon through the hole, and tie the ends together to create a hanger.

Gingerbread Houses for All

Celebrate the fun of making gingerbread by hosting a gingerbread decorating party and inviting student family members to join in the fun. Make individual houses using clean pint-size milk cartons, icing, and candies. Staple the top of each carton closed and secure it to a heavy duty paper plate with a dab of icing. Provide bowls of white icing and cover the outsides of the cartons. Attach graham cracker sections into the icing to resemble miniature gingerbread houses. Use a variety of candies, such as gum drops and candy dots, for decoration. To add decorations, place icing on each candy piece and attach it to the house. When the houses are finished, copy a gingerbread man pattern (page 24) on brown paper for each student. Photograph students with their handmade houses and place their photos on the gingerbread patterns as keepsakes of the special day.

22

Sugar and Spice Wreath

These gingerbread and candy cane wreathes will look good enough to eat! Let each student cut out the center of a paper plate. Trace reduced copies of the gingerbread man pattern (page 24) on brown grocery bags and cut out. Trace reduced copies of the candy cane patterns (page 24) on white construction paper. Decorate the gingerbread men and candy canes. Glue the patterns, along with peppermint swirl candies, randomly on the plate rim. Finish by punching a hole at the top and thread with yarn to create a hanger.

Trail of Sweets

Take a trip through a land of gingerbread and peppermint with this game. Bring in a new cookie sheet and several large magnets. Color and cut out copies of the gingerbread man, candy cane, and gingerbread house game pieces (page 25). To make game markers, glue the gingerbread men to the magnets. On the left side of the cookie sheet, glue a candy cane pattern labeled *Start*. On the right side, glue a gingerbread house pattern labeled *Finish*. Create a path from the candy cane to the gingerbread house by attaching self-adhesive colored dots. Decorate the gameboard (cookie sheet) by gluing on gumdrops. Two children at a time may play, each using a gingerbread man marker. Allow students to take turns rolling a die and moving the appropriate number of spaces. For older students, write phrases like *Move ahead one* or *Lose a turn* on some dots. For younger students, use a multicolored die and have them move to the color shown. The first person to reach the gingerbread house is the winner. Reward game winners with gumdrops and peppermint swirls.

Make Your Own Gingerbread

After learning about gingerbread, make and decorate gingerbread cookies using the recipe at right. You can make the recipe with the class or make it ahead of time.

Sift together the flour, baking soda, salt, and spices. Cut the butter into the flour in a large bowl until mixture resembles bread crumbs. Add the sugar, syrup, and egg yolk. Mix until dough is formed. Knead lightly. Wrap and chill dough for 30 minutes before shaping. Roll dough to 1/4" thickness and cut using cookie cutters. Bake at 350° for 12 minutes or until cookies begin to color around the edges. Provide tubes of colored icing and small candies for students to use to decorate the cookies. Place the cookies in plastic bags and attach gingerbread man tags with ribbon. Let students give their cookies as holiday gifts.

Gingerbread Cookies
1 1/4 cups all-purpose flour
1/4 teaspoon baking soda
Pinch of salt
1 teaspoon ground ginger
1 teaspoon ground cinnamon
5 tablespoons sweet butter
   cut into pieces
1/2 cup superfine sugar
2 tablespoons maple syrup
1 egg yolk, beaten

23

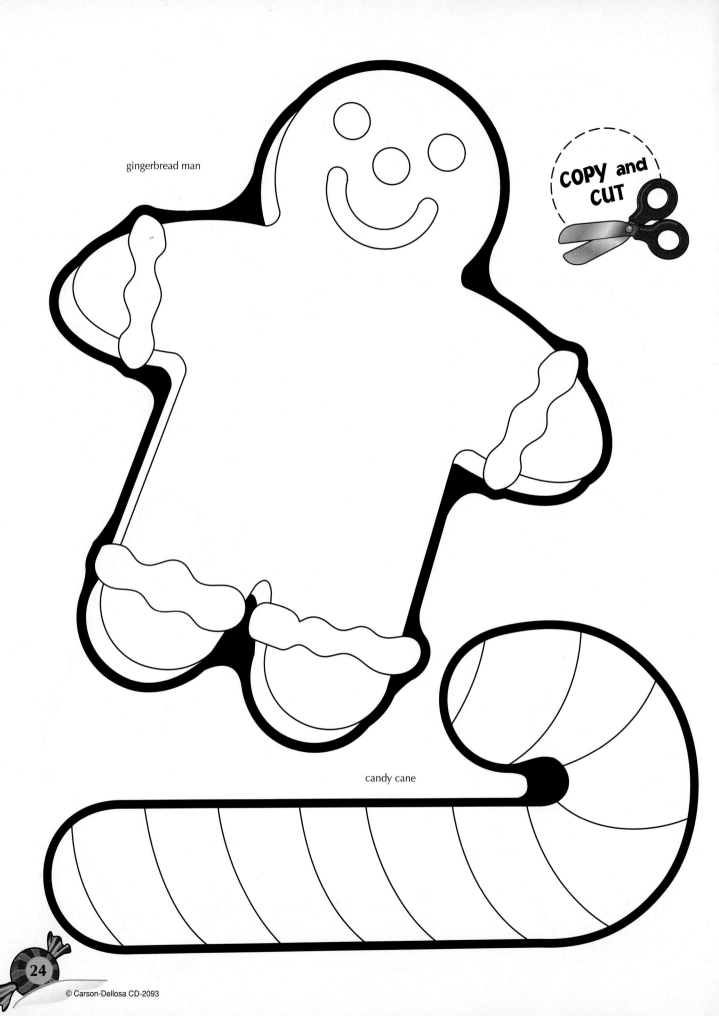

gingerbread man

COPY and CUT

candy cane

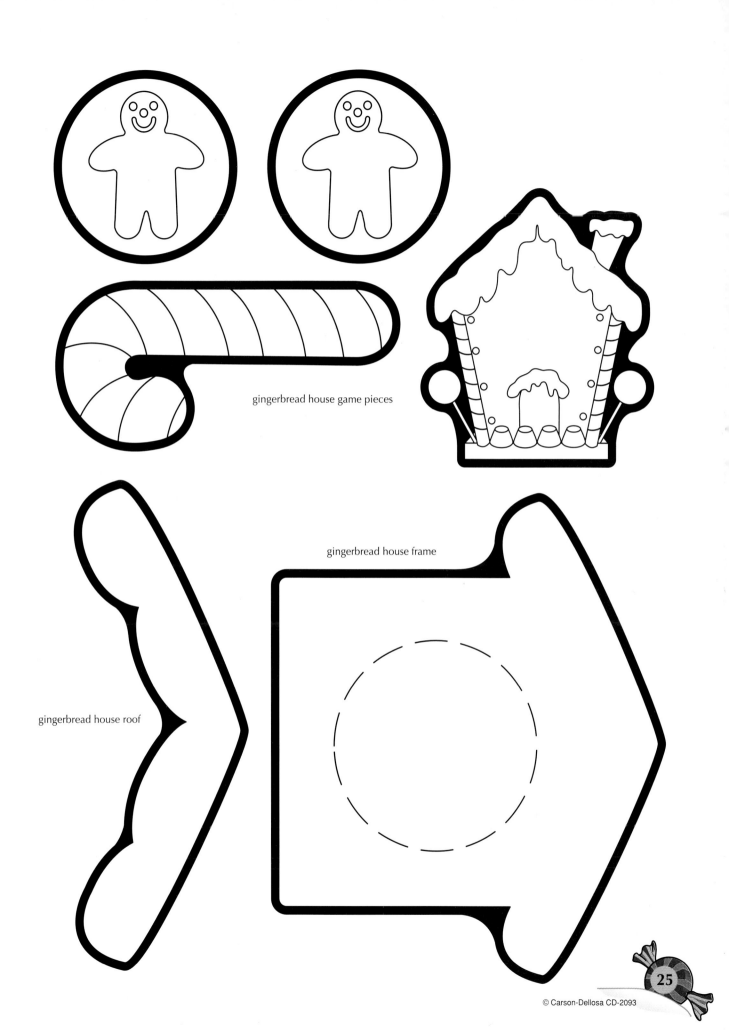

gingerbread house game pieces

gingerbread house frame

gingerbread house roof

25

HANUKKAH FESTIVAL OF LIGHTS

Hanukkah (HA•nah•kah) is an eight-day Jewish celebration also known as *The Festival of Lights*. It begins on the twenty-fifth day of the Hebrew month of *Kislev*, which falls in November or December. Hanukkah celebrates the victory of a small group of Jewish soldiers, led by *Judah Maccabbee* (MA•cah•bee), fighting for religious freedom. Their victory is known as the first miracle of Hanukkah.

When the Jewish soldiers reclaimed their Temple, they began to rebuild it. They searched for oil to light the *menorah* (meh•NOR•uh), a special oil lamp with several branches, but only found enough to last for a day. Miraculously, the menorah burned for eight days. This became known as the second miracle of Hanukkah. Jewish people celebrate Hanukkah by lighting candles on a menorah to symbolize the eight days the menorah was aglow at the Temple.

A Hanukkah celebration often includes storytelling, gift-giving, special foods, and games. *Dreidel* (DREY•duhl), a popular game using a four-sided spinning top, is played, and *latkes* (LAT•kehs), potato pancakes fried in oil, are served to symbolize the oil found in the Temple.

Hanukkah Activity Book

As you begin your class Hanukkah celebration, have students make Hanukkah activity books to note special things about the holiday. Give each child a yellow file folder. Color and cut out a copy of the menorah pattern (page 33). Glue the pattern to the folder and add gold glitter to the candles. Have students write their names and the date on the covers. Punch two holes through the folder, thread yarn through the holes, and tie. On squares of paper, draw or write about Hanukkah experiences. Glue the squares inside the book. Share the books at the end of the unit.

Literature Selections

Herschel and the Hanukkah Goblins by Eric A. Kimmel: Holiday House, 1994. (Picture book, 30 pg.) Herschel arrives in a village to find the people are not celebrating Hanukkah because their synagogue is haunted by goblins. He thinks of an ingenious way to rid the townspeople of the pesky goblins.

Latkes and Applesauce: A Hanukkah Story by Fran Manushkin: Scholastic Trade, 1992. (Picture book, 32 pg.) A family is unable to enjoy potato latkes on Hanukkah because of a blizzard. When they share the small amount of food they have with a puppy and a kitten, they get something special in return.

Hanukkah Lights, Hanukkah Nights by Leslie Kimmelman: HarperTrophy, 1994. (Picture book, 24 pg.) An entire family enjoys the traditions and customs of Hanukkah.

On Hanukkah by Cathy G. Fishman: Atheneum, 1998. (Picture book, 40 pg.) Follows a young girl and her family as they celebrate Hanukkah.

Inside-Out Grandma: A Hanukkah Story by Joan Rothenberg: Hyperion Books, 1995. (Picture book, 32 pg.) Grandma explains her unusual way of remembering to buy enough oil to make potato latkes for the Hanukkah celebration.

A Special Hanukkiah

The menorah used at home during Hanukkah is called a *hanukkiah* (HA•nah•KEE•ah). A hanukkiah has nine candles— eight candles for the eight nights of Hanukkah and one extra candle, called a shammash (sha•MAHSH), that is used to light the others. The shammash is set higher than the rest of the candles. The celebration begins by lighting the shammash and using it to light one candle on the first night, two candles on the second, and so on until all eight candles are lit on the last night. Each child can construct a hanukkiah using cardboard tubes and craft sticks. Glue a piece of construction paper around the tube. Cut nine small slits across the top of each student's tube with a craft knife. Allow students to decorate using markers and color nine craft sticks to look like candles. Cut orange paper flames and glue them to the tops of the candles. Slide a candle into each of the slits and raise the shammash slightly higher than the others. Glue the tube to an upside-down cup to create a stand. Display during your Hanukkah celebration.

Spin A Dreidel

Dreidel is a traditional Hanukkah game. A different Hebrew letter is shown on each side of the dreidel, which means "A great miracle happened there." Have students make dreidels using pint-sized milk or juice cartons and sharpened pencils. Open the top of the carton and use a craft knife to cut a small opening in the middle of the carton bottom. Slide a pencil through the carton so the point pokes through the hole. Staple the top closed around the pencil. Cut out the Hebrew letter patterns (page 34) and glue one letter to each side of the carton in the order nun, gimmel, hey, shin from right to left. Spin the dreidel by standing it up on the pencil point. Explain the rules of the game (see below) and have students take turns using their dreidels to play. Begin by having small groups sit in circles with an equal number of candy, buttons, or nuts. Each player puts a piece in the middle. Children take turns spinning the dreidel and following the directions based on which letter appears. The game ends when one player wins all of the pieces.

Nun—The player does nothing. The dreidel is spun again.
Gimmel—The player takes everything in the middle. Everyone puts in another piece before the next spin.
Hey—The player takes half of the pieces if there is an even amount or half plus one if there is an uneven amount.
Shin—The player puts in one piece.
Display the following key to help students remember the symbols:

N—nothing   H—half
G—get   Sh—share one

Add It Up!

Test your students' math skills with this variation of the dreidel game. Explain that the Hebrew letters on the dreidel also stand for numbers. Display the key below and have students take turns spinning the dreidel and adding their scores. The winner is the person who reaches 1,000 first.

Nun — 50
Gimmel — 3
Hey — 5
Shin — 300

A Dreidel So Sweet

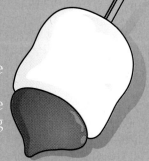

These sweet dreidels make the perfect Hanukkah treat. Slide a marshmallow onto the top of a blunt wooden toothpick. Add a chocolate candy kiss, pointed side out, as the dreidel top. Serve these delicious treats during your class Hanukkah celebration.

Dreidel Card

Deliver Hanukkah greetings with this clever dreidel card. Copy and cut out two dreidel patterns (page 33) from construction paper. Decorate one side of each using markers and crayons. Place the patterns together with the decorated sides facing out. Glue the bottom and sides together, leaving the top open. Cut a strip of oaktag about 1¹/₂" wide and write a Hanukkah greeting in the center. Slide the strip between the patterns. Label the top of the strip with the word *Pull*. The person who receives the card pulls the top of the dreidel to read the Hanukkah message inside.

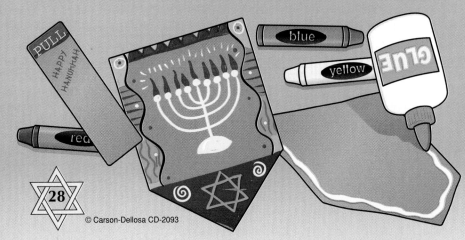

Homemade Potato Latkes

Potato latkes and other foods fried in oil are traditionally eaten during Hanukkah. Follow the recipe below to make homemade latkes.

3-4 pounds potatoes, grated
1 medium onion for each pound of potatoes, grated
1 egg
1½ teaspoons salt
½ teaspoon pepper
2 heaping tablespoons matzo meal or flour (or just
    enough to hold the mixture together)
Vegetable oil for frying

Mix the potatoes and onions together. Add egg, salt, pepper, and matzo meal or flour. Drop mixture by spoonfuls onto a hot, well-oiled skillet and flatten to make pancakes. Fry on both sides until golden brown. When cooked, drain the latkes on flattened brown paper grocery bags. Serve the latkes warm topped with applesauce and sour cream. Makes about 24 latkes.

Flipping Over Latkes

Your students will flip over this Hanukkah game. Give each student a small paper or plastic plate and glue a craft stick to the back. Then, have each child cut a 2" circle from poster board and decorate it to resemble a latke. Write the word *Happy* on one side and *Hanukkah* on the other. Punch a hole in the edge of the plate and the edge of the latke. Attach the latke to the plate by tying yarn through the holes. To play the game, flip the latke over and over until the words *Happy* and *Hanukkah* appear in order.

A Different Kind of Doughnut

Sufganiyot (SOOF•gan•ee•yoat) are jelly doughnuts sprinkled with sugar and served as Hanukkah treats. Children can make miniature sufganiyot using doughnut holes, jelly, and powdered sugar. Cut the doughnut holes in half and spread a small amount of jelly on one side of each piece. Put the pieces together and sprinkle with powdered sugar. Enjoy!

Special Gelt Holders

Legend states that after the Jewish soldiers repaired the Temple and relit the menorah, they made new coins for the Jewish people, which may be how giving *gelt* (the Yiddish word for money) became a Hanukkah tradition. Children often receive foil-covered chocolate coins or actual money as Hanukkah gelt. Make a gelt holder with a paper plate and a paper plate half. Provide markers, crayons, and glitter. Let children decorate the plates with Hanukkah symbols. Staple or glue the paper plate half to the bottom of the paper plate to create a pocket. Fill the gelt holders with chocolate coins or create your own special treats using the suggestions below.

Gelt Treats

Here are some fun snacks that can be used as gelt.

- Melt several chocolate bars according to the package directions. Pour small dollops of chocolate onto a cookie sheet covered with wax paper. Place in the refrigerator to set. Wrap the hardened candies in gold foil.
- Wrap mini cookies in yellow plastic wrap. Secure with clear tape, if necessary.
- Tint cake frosting using yellow food coloring. Spread the frosting between two vanilla wafer cookies to create a tasty gelt treat.

Tzedakah Container

Often, money given as gifts during Hanukkah is placed in a *tzedakah* (tsah•DAH•kah) container. Money collected is donated to charity. It is customary to put coins in a tzedakah container on the eve of various Jewish holidays throughout the year. Children can make tzedakah containers and donate Hanukkah gelt. Cover a small container with a lid (such as a cake frosting container) with construction paper. Cut a small coin slot in the container lid. Draw and cut out Hanukkah symbols, such as gelt, Stars of David, dreidels, and menorahs from felt and glue them to the sides of the container. Decorate the symbols using sequins and yarn. Encourage children to think of ways they can use the coins collected to help others.

It's Hanukkah Time!

Blue, white, and yellow are colors associated with Hanukkah. Blue and white are the colors of the Israeli flag and yellow represents the glow of the Hanukkah candles. Copy the dreidel, Star of David, and menorah patterns (page 33). Have students decorate the patterns with markers, glitter, and tissue paper. Make a paper chain using blue, white, and yellow strips of construction paper which have been made into loops. Attach the decorated patterns to the chain using string or thread.

30

Celebrate With Poetry

The brightly lit menorah is the focus of the Hanukkah celebration. Write the letters from the word Hanukkah in each candle flame on the menorah pattern (page 33). Write a Hanukkah-related word or phrase on each arm of the menorah beginning with the letter shown in the candle flame above it. Combine the poems to create a Hanukkah book.

HANUKKAH

H — Holiday when
A — All eight candles burn brightly
N — Nighttime is when we celebrate
U — Until 8 days
K — keep stories
K — kisses and
A — Always good food to eat
H — Hanukkah is a time to celebrate

play dreidel
eat latkes
gelt
Hanukkah
light the menorah
give gifts
Read stories

Sights and Sounds of Hanukkah

What are the traditions and customs of Hanukkah? Have each student draw a large Star of David on a sheet of paper. Write Hanukkah in the center of the pattern and a Hanukkah custom or tradition on each star point. Create an *All About Hanukkah* display by posting the projects on a bulletin board.

Happy Hanukkah Cards

Students can extend warm Hanukkah greetings with these sparkling holiday cards. Have students cut two large triangles from yellow paper. Outline the edges of each with white glue and sprinkle with gold glitter. When the glue has dried, turn one triangle upside-down and use clear tape to adhere the bottom edge to the middle of the other triangle, forming a Star of David. Lift the top triangle and write Happy Hanukkah greetings on the bottom triangle.

Happy Hanukkah!
From, Leah

for Jake

The Sweetest Gift

Hanukkah is a holiday for family togetherness. Create unique applesauce jars, complete with recipe cards and encourage students to take them home and work with a family member to make the recipe. To make the jar, have each student glue pieces of fabric, wallpaper scraps, etc., to a small plastic container with a lid, such as a peanut butter jar. Give each student a copy of the applesauce recipe card (page 35) to color and cut out. When the container is dry, place the recipe cards inside. Cut a piece of fabric to cover the lid and secure it using a rubber band. Attach the Applesauce Poem (page 35) to the lid with yarn. Children can give these jars as Hanukkah gifts.

Latkes are a Hanukkah treat
Topped with applesauce, oh so sweet.
The sweetest topping has to be,
Applesauce made by you and me.
Happy Hanukkah!
Love,
Trish

Hanukkah Frames

Enjoy Hanukkah memories all year long with these festive frames. Give each student twelve craft sticks. Place two sticks side-by-side on top of two others, overlapping and gluing the ends to make a triangle. Make another triangle from the remaining sticks. Glue one triangle to the other to make a Star of David. Cut a piece of construction paper to fit the opening in the center. Glue a photograph or draw a picture on the paper, then glue the edges to the back of the frame. If desired, glue a piece of yarn to the top for hanging.

Festive Gift Wrap

Children can wrap their homemade Hanukkah gifts in handmade holiday gift bags. Provide white paper lunch bags along with cookie cutters in a variety of Hanukkah shapes. Paint the edges of a cookie cutter. Gently press the cookie cutter on the paper to make a print. When dry, use markers to personalize the gift bag. Place a Hanukkah gift inside, fold down, and punch two holes in the top. Thread ribbon through the holes and tie. Present these gifts to someone special during Hanukkah.

HAPPY HANUKKAH
to: Matt
from: Dez

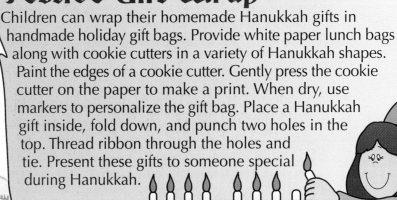

32

dreidel

COPY and CUT

Star of David

menorah

33

Shin

Hey

Nun

Gimmel

Homemade Applesauce

6 apples peeled, cored, and cut into chunks
Juice from half a lemon
$\frac{1}{2}$ cup water
$\frac{1}{4}$ cup sugar
1 teaspoon cinnamon

Place apples in a saucepan. Add lemon juice and water. Bring to a boil. Reduce heat to low and cover. Cook for 30 minutes or until apples are soft. Add cinnamon and sugar before serving.

COPY and CUT

Latkes are a Hanukkah treat
Topped with applesauce, oh so sweet.
The sweetest topping has to be,
Applesauce made by you and me.
Happy Hanukkah!
Love,

_____

Applesauce Poem

35

ANIMALS IN WINTER

Animals adapt to winter weather in a variety of ways—some hibernate, some migrate, and others stay busy looking for food. This unit illustrates how different animals spend the long winter months and how we can help them throughout the season.

DID YOU KNOW?

❄ When some animals hibernate, they go into a deep sleep and cannot be awakened easily. Their breathing and heartbeats slow down and their body temperatures drop severely to conserve energy.

❄ Many animals build up a layer of fat and develop thicker coats to keep warm during the cold winter. The winter coats of some animals, such as the snowshoe hare and the ermine, turn white to hide them in the snow from predators.

❄ Animals that forage for food during winter are most active in the afternoon, when the day is warmest.

LITERATURE SELECTIONS

Backyard Birds of Winter by Carol Lerner: William Morrow & Co., 1994. (Reference book, 48 pg.) A beginner bird watching handbook for young children, including pictures and descriptions of over 40 of the most common species of winter birds.

In the Snow: Who's Been Here by Lindsay Barret George: Greenwillow Books, 1995. (Picture book, 40 pg.) Visual and written clues are given for several animals that left traces behind in the snow. A turn of the page reveals each animal.

Crinkleroot's Book of Animal Tracks and Wildlife Signs by Jim Arnosky: Putnam Publishing Group, 1979. (Reference book, 47 pg.) A friendly mountain man points out signs of animals in the wild and provides information about their behaviors.

Animals in Winter by Henrietta Bancroft and Richard G. Van Gelder: Harper Collins Juvenile Books, 1997. (Reference book, 32 pg.) Explores the many ways animals prepare for winter and offers suggestions for how humans can help.

DEAR DIARY

Discuss the winter behavior of animals. Break students into small groups and assign an animal to each group. Provide encyclopedias and books about animals for reference. Each member should write a diary entry telling how the animal spends winter, using adjectives to describe the animal's surroundings, nesting habits, and food gathering. Bind each group's entries together into a booklet, and label it with the animal's name, for example, *Bear's Winter Journal*. Let each group read and act out their journal entries, then place the books at a reading center.

36

ANIMALS ADAPT (AND SO DO WE!)

Talk about how animals adapt to winter weather. Name several animals and have the class tell how they adapt to winter. Compare these behaviors to what humans do in winter. Let students fold a piece of paper in half horizontally. On one side, write and illustrate a sentence about how an animal changes in winter. On the other side, write and illustrate how a person adapts to winter in a similar way. For example, *A squirrel's tail becomes bushier to keep it warm* and *I wear a heavy winter coat to keep me warm*. Let older students write analogies, such as *squirrel is to tail as human is to coat*. Display these illustrations with the title *Human Animals in Winter.*

CREATURE COMFORTS

The comforts of home to a chipmunk are leaves and nuts, but to humans, the comforts of home include televisions, soft blankets, and puffy pillows. Imagine having to hibernate one winter. Have students write stories including details such as where to hibernate, what to eat in preparation for the long sleep, what to keep in the den all winter, what to do to fall asleep, etc. Let students illustrate hibernating in that special spot, then share their stories with the class.

winter animal poems

Describe an animal in winter with these quick three-line poems. For the first line, have students write two adjectives describing an animal. Write a phrase describing what the animal does during winter for the second line, and write the animal's name for the third line. Have students write final copies on animal patterns (pages 48-51) and cut out. Read the first two lines of a poem and challenge the class to guess the animal before the last line is read. Display the poems on a bulletin board.

Big, furry
Sleeps through the winter
Bear

CATERPILLAR METEOROLOGIST

12

What do a caterpillar and groundhog have in common? They are both said to predict winter weather. The groundhog is the most famous weather forecaster, but folklore tells of other weather savvy animals. It is said that the wider the brown band on a wooly bear caterpillar, the harsher the winter will be. Have students write winter weather reports, given by wooly bear caterpillars. Draw a picture of a television screen. Create the caterpillar with thick pipe cleaners, cutting the length of the pipe cleaners to adjust the amount of brown and black so that the wooly bear reflects the weather report. (For example, if the wooly bear were giving a report of a very severe winter, he would have a very wide brown section in the middle, and just a little black on the ends.) Twist the black pipe cleaner sections to the brown pipe cleaner at the ends and coil around a pencil. Glue the wooly bear caterpillar to the television screen and draw a speech balloon with his winter forecast report inside.

This winter will be long and cold.

37

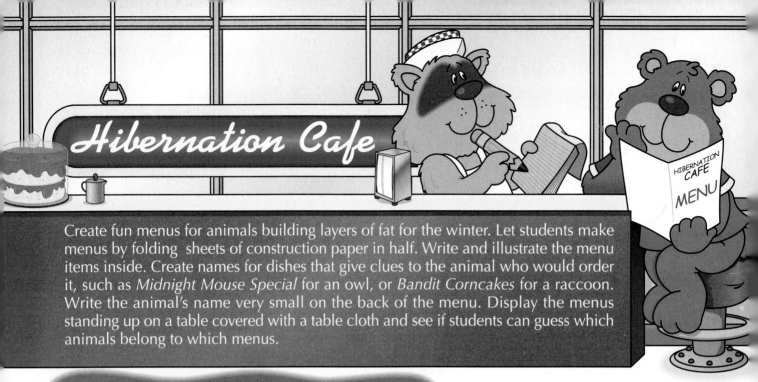

Hibernation Cafe

Create fun menus for animals building layers of fat for the winter. Let students make menus by folding sheets of construction paper in half. Write and illustrate the menu items inside. Create names for dishes that give clues to the animal who would order it, such as *Midnight Mouse Special* for an owl, or *Bandit Corncakes* for a raccoon. Write the animal's name very small on the back of the menu. Display the menus standing up on a table covered with a table cloth and see if students can guess which animals belong to which menus.

FORAGING CENTERS

Give students the chance to behave like animals! Let them pretend to be foraging animals such as deer, rabbits, and squirrels, which spend their winter days looking for food. Food is scarce in the winter because many plants die or lose their leaves. Other food is hidden underground and under the snow. Foraging animals must be alert and gather food quickly so they can return to their homes where it is warm and safe from predators. Set up two tables with several boxes. In the boxes at one table, hide 20 acorns or acorn patterns (page 49) under shredded brown paper ("dirt"). At the other table, hide 20 leaves or pictures of leaves in the boxes, under white shredded paper ("snow"). Then, display a picture of a tree on the wall. Tape 20 strips of brown paper ("bark") sparingly to the tree. Divide the class into three teams, deer, rabbits, and squirrels. Let students work for three minutes to gather all 20 pieces of their animals' food. (Food for squirrels=acorns, rabbits=leaves under the snow, and deer=bark and tree leaves). The first team to gather all 20 pieces of its food and return "home" (to their desks) wins. Let the groups trade animal names and play until each group has been all three animals. After all of the "animals" have found their food, have a real snack (see *Paw Print Cakes*, page 44) and talk about the challenges that animals face during the winter.

YOU ARE WHAT YOU EAT

Many animals eat plenty of food in preparation for the winter. After learning about the variety of foods animals eat, have students create these expressive collages. Have each child draw an outline of an animal, or trace an animal pattern (pages 48-51). Cut out magazine pictures of things the animal might eat and glue them inside the outline. Real objects, such as nuts, corn kernels, grass, etc., can be glued on as well. When the animals are completely covered, cut them out. On a piece of butcher paper, draw a forest scene and sponge paint the scene with white paint for snow. Glue the animals to the scene to complete the project.

38

ENERGY MELT-DOWN

The science behind hibernation has to do with how fast animals "burn" their energy supply. People and animals get energy from the foods they eat and can store the energy in their bodies as fat. Explain that when people and other mammals are busy and active, they get hot and "burn" energy faster. Point out how students feel warm when they use energy to run and play. When they are sleeping, people and other mammals cool off and burn less energy. (This is why people need covers on their beds at night!) Hibernating animals live on the energy in their fat and do not need to eat all winter. Demonstrate this principle to students with butter and water. Display two clear jars (with lids), one labeled *Active* and another labeled *Hibernation*. Put hot water in the *Active* jar, and cold water in the *Hibernation* jar. Drop a pat of butter into each jar to represent an animal's stored fat. Tightly close the lids on each jar and gently shake the *Active* jar, to simulate an animal's activity, and let the *Hibernation* jar sit still. Show students how the hot, active water used the stored energy very quickly while the cold, still water did not use up the fat or stored energy.

CUDDLE UP

As an animal hibernates, its temperature drops dramatically to keep it from using up its stored fat too quickly. However, if its temperature drops too low, it will die. So, if the animal's temperature starts to get too low, it wakes up so it can warm up to a safe temperature. Hibernating animals sleep curled up in a ball shape to keep them from getting too cold. Have each student make a fist with one hand and hold the other flat, away from her body. After thirty seconds, have her place each hand on her face and compare the difference in temperatures. Compare the two hands to a hibernating animal and decide which sleeping position is best for keeping warm.

WINTER WEIGHT

Lose weight while you sleep? The only catch is you have to sleep for three months! Bears and other hibernating animals use up the fat they added in the fall while they sleep, waking up slim, trim, and hungry in spring. Have students make interactive storybooks about bears fattening up for winter and slimming down during hibernation. Let each child write a short story about a bear eating different foods and getting ready for winter. Throughout the story, indicate places where the reader can add or take away fat (cotton balls) from the bear. Trace a bear pattern (page 48) onto brown felt and cut it out. Fold a sheet of construction paper in half so the fold is at the top, write the title on the front, and staple the story inside. To glue the felt bear above the story, glue around the edges and do not press it flat, but pull it out to create a small pocket. Staple a small resealable bag to the back of the book and add 4-6 cotton balls, depending on how many were indicated in the story. Have students exchange stories and follow the directions in each book for fattening up and slimming down the bears.

Barney Bear was hungry! It was almost time for his long winter nap, so he had to hurry up and find food. He caught a few fish and ate them (add 2 cotton balls). Barney decided to catch some more fish. He ate until he was full (add 1 cotton ball).

39

COAT COVER UPS

Animals need winter coats, but not the kind with buttons and hoods. Most mammals grow a winter coat of thick fur in preparation for the cold winter. Let students color an animal pattern (pages 48-51). Draw a winter scene on construction paper and glue the animal to the picture. Glue brown or black yarn on top of the animal, following its outline, until it is completely covered with its new winter coat. If an animal like the snowshoe hare is chosen, use white yarn since its fur grows in white in winter.

WINTER BRRRR-OWS

Dig deep to create an intricate burrow of hibernation rooms and tunnels. Many hibernating animals make their winter homes by tunneling underground. The burrows may be simple holes or elaborate sets of tunnels. Have students roll down the top edges of brown paper lunch bags two or three times and place the bags on their sides to form cross sections of a burrow. Decorate the "burrows" with dried leaves, raffia, twigs, etc. Staple the bags to a bulletin board and cut black construction paper to form tunnels connecting the sections. Color and cut out a groundhog pattern (page 48) and a chipmunk pattern (page 50) to place inside the burrows. Title the display *Shh! Hibernating Animals!*

COOL CAMOUFLAGE

Show how white animals can hide in the snow with this simple science experiment. Pair students and give each a handful of red, yellow, and white paper squares, approximately 1" x 1", and a large sheet of white paper. Let one student sprinkle the squares on the paper and tell the other to pick up as many squares as possible in 30 seconds. After time is up, sort the squares that were picked up and count the number of squares of each color. Have students switch roles and try the experiment again. Talk about how the white squares were camouflaged on the white paper like white animals are camouflaged in the snow. As an extension activity, have students complete the *Hidden Animals* worksheet (page 47).

SHH! HIBERNATING ANIMALS!

LONG WINTER'S NAP

It would be nice to stay in bed on a cold winter day! Animals, like the skunk, raccoon, and opossum do. They alternate between sleeping and wakefulness during the winter. They are not true hibernators, but are winter nappers. These animals sleep during the harshest weather, and wake during milder weather to forage for food. Illustrate napping wintertime animals using construction paper and crayons. Let students fold the edges of a piece of light-colored construction paper to meet in the middle. Draw a burrow, log, or other sleeping place on the outside of the folded paper. Open the paper and draw a napping animal inside surrounded by leaves, twigs, etc. Write *Do Not Disturb–Napping* on a small square of paper, attach a piece of yarn, and tape it to the front of the paper.

DO NOT DISTURB napping

FEED THE BEAR

Feed this hungry bear with facts. Write true or false statements about animals in winter on blueberry patterns (page 49), and write *true* or *false* on the back of each pattern. Enlarge, color, and cut out two bear face patterns (page 48) and glue each to an empty cereal box. Have an adult cut out the mouth of each bear. To play *Feed the Bear*, divide the class into two teams and give each team a box. Let teams take turns picking patterns and reading the statements. Have a student decide if the statement is true or false and check the back of the pattern for the answer. If the answer is correct, a point is earned, and the pattern is placed in the team's box. Continue play until each fact has been read. When the game is complete, have each team count its blueberries. The team with the most blueberries wins. Have a snack of blueberries to congratulate the winning team.

MAPPING MIGRATION

SAN JUAN CAPESTRANO UNITED STATES

To avoid the cold and lack of food during winter, some animals migrate, or move to warmer climates. Divide the class into groups of three and let each group research a migrating animal such as gray whales, reindeer, Canada geese, monarch butterflies, or robins. Have the groups make quick reference cards for their animals, including information about where, when, and why the animals migrate. Have groups draw small pictures of their animals, tape strips of paper to the backs, and thread yarn between the strips and the drawings. Display a world map and let each group tape its reference card to the map, near the animal's summer home, and attach a length of yarn from the animal's summer home to its winter home. Slide the drawing back and forth on the yarn, so that the animal can "migrate" between its two homes.

ANGANGUEO MEXICO

41

BIRD WATCHING JOURNAL

There are several species of birds that stay in the same place all year long and forage for food in winter. It is easy to observe these birds if you offer them food and water near a window. (See page 45 for bird feeder ideas.) Let students keep a record of the birds seen in winter. Have each student fold and staple several sheets of white paper into a journal. Color several bird patterns (page 49) to look like local, non-migrating birds. Some examples may include the cardinal, chickadee, blue jay, nuthatch, etc. Cut out the patterns and glue one on each page of the journal. Keep the journals at a special bird watching station beside a window, along with binoculars and books about birds. Hang a bird feeder outside the window. When a bird comes to feed, ask students to name it. Let each child record the name of the bird on the appropriate page of her journal, including the date and a short sentence describing what the bird was doing.

"V" IS FOR GEESE

Birds of a feather flock together—in a V-formation. Many birds fly south during the winter to escape the cold air and lack of food. Some birds, like Canada Geese, fly in a V-shaped formation to reduce the force of the wind on the geese behind them. Cut several sponges into the shapes of flying birds. Fill several shallow containers with white and black tempera paint. Dip part of a sponge in black paint and part in white paint and press them onto dark blue construction paper to create birds. Arrange the birds in a V-shape, resembling a flock of migrating Canada Geese. Arrange the pictures in a V-formation on a wall or bulletin board.

HIBERNATION HIDE AND SEEK

Insects and cold-blooded animals such as frogs and turtles hibernate in the winter because they cannot warm their bodies on their own. In winter their body temperatures would fall below freezing and they would die. Have students create hide-and-seek books to reveal hibernating cold-blooded animals. Draw a different scene on each page of a booklet, including a cross section of a pond, a pile of leaves, rocks, a tree trunk, and a house. Then, cut a mud puddle for the pond, a leaf, a rock, some bark, and the house from construction paper. Tape the top of each object to its appropriate page. Lift each object and draw a frog, turtle, ladybug, etc., under the object. Write a fact about each animal or insect at the top of the page. If desired, share the completed booklets with another class.

THINK SPRING

This animal hides under the mud to hibernate.

BIG ANIMAL TRACKS

Make a real impression with this animal track activity. Cut various animal tracks from cardboard, using the animal tracks (page 46) as reference. Glue a stick, pencil, or marker upright to the back of each cut out and place them on a table. Put plaster of paris in plastic foam bowls. Let a few students at a time come to the table, choose a track, identify the animal using the reference, and press it into the plaster, creating a print. Let the plaster harden completely. Display the impressions on a table covered with quilt batting "snow" along with picture cards or names of animals. Let students try to match the prints with the correct animals.

WHO WAS HERE?

Be animal detectives! Explain that animals leave behind clues that tell us they have been there, such as tracks in the snow, food not eaten, pieces of materials gathered to add to their nests, holes dug, etc. Show animal tracks (page 46) and let each student choose one. Have students use inkpads and their fingerprints to create animal tracks on a piece of white paper. Have them make several prints, creating a trail of tracks across the page. After the tracks are printed, have students draw bits of nut shells, bark stripped from trees, etc., to give clues to the animal that made the tracks. On the back of each paper, have each child draw a picture of the animal that made the prints. Bind the pictures into a class book titled *Who Was Here?* and let students use the clues to detect which animal walked along which page.

DON'T WAKE THE BEAR

When a bear hibernates, it can be easily awakened. Play a fun game of tag by trying not to wake the sleeping bear (he might be grumpy!). Choose a child to be the sleeping bear. Have him sit on the ground and cover his face, pretending to be asleep. Draw a line with masking tape halfway between the "bear" and the other students. Let the other children tiptoe up to the bear and ask "Are you sleeping?" If the bear answers "Yes," the children tiptoe away and return to the other side of the room. If the bear answers "No!," the bear jumps up and tries to tag a child, but cannot go out of his cave (beyond the line). If the bear tags a classmate, that student becomes the bear. If the bear does not tag a classmate, he goes back to sleep and the game continues.

43

ACORN OR OAK TREE

Many foraging animals spend the fall season collecting and storing food in their burrows for the winter months. Squirrels bury acorns in the ground to be retrieved in the winter. Although many of the nuts are found and dug up, some remain in the ground because squirrels forget where they buried them! Some of these forgotten nuts grow to be oak trees. Choose one child to be the "squirrel" and have her give a copy of the acorn pattern (page 49) to three different students. Then, have the squirrel leave the room or turn her back while those three students give the acorns to three other students (making the squirrel "forget" where she put the acorns). The squirrel has three chances to find the acorns. She should go around the "forest" (the classroom) and lightly tap a child's hand. If the child has an acorn, he gives it to the squirrel. If he does not, he simply reveals his empty hand and silently shakes his head. After the squirrel has had three chances, invite any student still holding an acorn to grow into an oak tree by standing and spreading out his arms like branches. Collect the acorns. Choose a new squirrel, and play again.

HELPING ANIMALS GUIDE

All animals need certain things to survive (food, water, air, shelter). Talk about how animals' needs, such as food and water, are harder to find in winter. Give each child four pieces of white paper and two colorful sheets for a front and back cover. Label the first page *Food*, the second page *Shelter*, and the third page *Water* (air is available.) For each category, let students cut out pictures from magazines of things humans can provide for animals. Pictures of cloth and yarn could be glued to the shelter page as examples of things a person could place in her yard to provide animals with warm materials to line their winter homes. Seeds, raffia, cloth scraps, and other craft items can be glued to each page, where appropriate. On the last page, draw a winter scene, and cut out magazine pictures of animals to glue to the scene in places they would be found in winter. Punch three holes along the left side of the pages and bind them together by threading raffia through the holes and knotting. Share the guides with another class to spread the word about helping animals in winter.

PAW PRINT CAKES

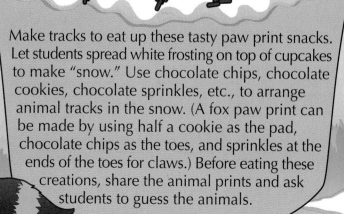

Make tracks to eat up these tasty paw print snacks. Let students spread white frosting on top of cupcakes to make "snow." Use chocolate chips, chocolate cookies, chocolate sprinkles, etc., to arrange animal tracks in the snow. (A fox paw print can be made by using half a cookie as the pad, chocolate chips as the toes, and sprinkles at the ends of the toes for claws.) Before eating these creations, share the animal prints and ask students to guess the animals.

44

FRUIT FEEDERS

Orange peels create a base for a natural bird feeder. Cut several oranges in half and scoop out the inside. Snack on the oranges while giving each student half of an orange rind. Have an adult use a sharp instrument to poke three holes evenly spaced around the edge of the rind. Tie a piece of string through each hole and tie them together at the top. Place bird seed in the orange feeders. Hang the feeders by the strings on tree branches for birds to enjoy.

STRING IT UP

Feed a variety of animals with these decorative food garlands. Provide blunt needles, heavy duty thread, and a selection of cut foods, such as cheese, popcorn, fruit, and raw vegetables. Have students thread the foods onto a length of string, tying each end in a knot when finished. The food garlands should be placed low in trees and bushes at home or at school to provide food for a variety of animals, including squirrels, deer, and raccoons.

WATER, WATER EVERYWHERE...

It may seem that with all the snow and ice there would be plenty of water for animals in winter. Animals, however, avoid eating ice and snow as their source of water because it takes too much energy to warm the snow inside their bodies. Help thirsty animals by making a simple water feeder. Have an adult hot glue a large plastic bowl onto the bottom of a plastic container such as an empty peanut butter jar. Place the feeder outside a classroom window by twisting the open container end into the ground. Fill the bowl with fresh water. Let students take turns putting fresh water in the bowl each day.

PEANUT BUTTER

45

raccoon

fox

deer

cotton tail
rabbit

chipmunk

pigeon

squirrel

groundhog

skunk

owl

bear

© Carson-Dellosa CD-2093

Name _____

Hidden Animals

Circle the hidden animals. Then, color the picture.

47

bear

COPY and CUT

groundhog

bear face

raccoon

bird

frog

turtle

blueberry

acorn

COPY and CUT

deer

rabbit

fox

chipmunk

squirrel

owl

mouse

skunk

51

Christmas
Throughout the World

In many countries, as in the United States, Christmas is a religious holiday celebrating the birth of Jesus Christ. The traditional Christmas story tells of Joseph and his pregnant wife, Mary, who traveled to Bethlehem. Since there was no room at the nearby inn, the couple stayed in a stable where the baby, Jesus, was born. Shepherds came to see the baby Jesus and wise men later came to Bethlehem and gave gifts to him. Customs and traditions for celebrating Christmas vary from country to country, but in any Christmas celebration, a festive and giving spirit is sure to be found. In this chapter, students will learn how Christmas is celebrated in Mexico, Germany, France, Italy, England, and Australia.

Literature Selections

Each of these books provides information and pictures of Christmas celebrations in various parts of the world.

Christmas Around the World by Emily Kelley: Carolrhoda Books, 1986. (Reference book, 46 pg.)

Christmas Around the World by Mary D. Lankford: William Morrow and Company, 1995. (Reference book, 47 pg.)

Christmas Gift Bringers by Leonard B. Lubin: Lothrop, Lee, & Shepard Books 1989. (Reference book, 32 pg.)

Fanciful Fireplace

Many families enjoy fires in their fireplaces during the Christmas season. The fireplace is also where Santa makes his entrance into homes in some Christmas traditions. Warm up your classroom during the Christmas season by creating a fireplace display for a wall or bulletin board. Throughout the holiday season, students can display their work, crafts, and tell stories by the "fire." Use white butcher paper for the background. Dip a rectangular sponge in red paint and print a brick pattern on the paper. When dry, attach the paper to a bulletin board. Glue a black paper square to the center. Enlarge a copy of the fireplace logs pattern (page 70), color, cut out, and glue inside the black square. To create a mantel, staple shoe boxes above the center black square. Let students add decorations, such as garland, wreaths, etc.

Christmas Gift Givers

Who brings toys to all the boys and girls around the world? That depends on where you live. Different countries have different gift givers. Read stories about the different gift givers to students and provide a brief description of each (see below).

Three Kings (Mexico)

The three kings ride camels.

Christkindl (Germany)

This child has golden wings and a flowing white gown and wears a jeweled crown.

Santa Claus (United States)

Santa is an old man with a big belly, white hair, and a beard. He wears a red suit with white fur trim, a black belt, and boots. He rides in a sleigh pulled through the sky by flying reindeer.

Père Noël (France)

Père Noël is an old man who wears a fur-trimmed robe. He has a beard and is like Father Christmas and Santa Claus.

La Befana (Italy)

La Befana is a crone-like old woman who wears a scarf on her head and rides a broom.

Father Christmas (England)

Father Christmas is a bearded giant who wears a fur-trimmed robe and a crown of holly.

Let students draw each gift giver based on the description, write the name of the country he or she is from, and a short paragraph about the gift giver. Glue the pictures to yellow construction paper, cutting a decorative pattern around the edges for frames. Display the framed work on a bulletin board. Place books about the gift givers nearby so children can compare their pictures to those in the books. To review each country's gift giver, have students complete the Gift Givers worksheet (page 68).

Christmas in the United States
"Merry Christmas"

Did You Know?

✦ Christmas traditions in the United States originated in many countries. The tradition of decorating a Christmas tree started in Germany. The customs of sending Christmas cards and caroling began in England.

✦ Children wait for Santa Claus to come to their houses on Christmas Eve. He arrives on a sleigh pulled by flying reindeer and fills stockings hung by the chimney with small gifts. One legend says that the custom of hanging stockings by the fire started one Christmas night when several coins fell out of Santa's pocket as he was going back up the chimney and landed inside socks that had been placed by the fire to dry.

Literature Selections

Christmas Time by Gail Gibbons: Holiday House, 1988. (Picture book, 32 pg.) A story about how and why we celebrate Christmas.

Everett Anderson's Christmas Coming by Lucile Clifton: Henry Holt & Company, 1991. (Picture book, 28 pg.) A young boy anticipates Christmas in the city.

Santa's Book of Names by David McPhail: Little Brown & Co., 1997. (Picture book, 32 pg.) Edward learns to read quickly when Santa asks him for help.

Christmas Tree Memories by Aliki: Harper-Trophy, 1994. (Picture book, 32 pg.) The family Christmas tree serves as a catalyst for Christmas memories.

The Night Before Christmas by Clement Clarke Moore: Little Brown & Co., 1999. (Picture book, 32 pg.) The classic tale of Santa's arrival.

Ask Santa

If you could ask Santa a question, what would it be? Cut out two stocking patterns (page 70) for each child and staple all edges but the top. Have each child write his name and a question for Santa, such as *What do you do with all the cookies people leave for you?* or *Who writes your naughty and nice list?,* on his stocking. Place the stockings in a bag or Santa cap. Let each child choose a question and write and illustrate an answer on a smaller copy of the stocking pattern as if he were Santa . Have each child place the answer from Santa inside the stocking. Display the stockings "hanging" from the *Fanciful Fireplace* (page 52). Let each student find his stocking and read Santa's answer.

Dear Tommy,

Tommy

Santa, How cold is it at the North Pole?

A Melting Pot Holiday

Explain to students that a melting pot is a combination of many traditions and cultures. Have students write and illustrate descriptions of special holiday traditions their families celebrate. Make sure the descriptions answer all the "w" questions (who, what, where, why, when, how). Bind the pages together in a class book. Let each child cut out two large pot shapes from black poster board for covers. Have students color small symbols from their traditions or flags from the countries where their traditions originated. Cut out the symbols and glue to the pots. Title the book *A Melting Pot Holiday* and share with the class.

Reindeer Research

Can reindeer really fly? Not without Santa's magic. Gather science books and nature magazines with information about reindeer. Have students find out where they live, what they eat, etc. Cut a piece of brown construction paper in half horizontally. Write reindeer facts on a piece of notebook paper. Cut the corners of the construction paper so that it is triangle-shaped. Cut and glue on construction paper facial features and antlers. Tape the top of the reindeer head to the writing paper to make a cute cover for the report.

Christmas Cookie Math

What's more fun than decorating Christmas cookies? Eating them! First, challenge students to change the recipe so there is enough for everyone. Write a basic cookie-cutter cookie recipe on chart paper and post. Let students work in pairs to halve the recipe, double it, divide it into thirds or fourths, and triple or quadruple it. Bring in undecorated cookies. Reward the class for their hard work by letting them decorate the cookies with frosting and sprinkles.

Santa's Helpers

Encourage students to be good helper elves in the classroom, just as Santa's elves help him at his workshop. Have each student trace the outline of his shoe on heavy stock paper and cut it out. Cut a red construction paper circle and glue it slightly above the middle of the shoe print to make a nose. Draw on eyes, a mouth, and color the cheeks rosy. To make each hat, cut a triangle, rectangle, and circle from red and white construction paper into long curved triangles, rectangles, and circles. Let each child glue the triangle on top of the rectangle and then glue the circle on top. Glue the hats on top of the shoe print faces, and have students write their names on the brims. Hang the elves on a bulletin board titled *Mrs. _____'s Little Helpers* and use the display as a job assignment.

Christmas in Mexico
"Feliz Navidad"
(fay•LEEZ na•vee•DAHD)

Did You Know?

◆ Most Mexican people decorate trees with lights, paper flowers, and pottery.

◆ Some people in Mexico exchange gifts on January 6, Epiphany Day, when it is believed that the three wise men brought gifts to the infant Jesus.

◆ Often, instead of stockings, Mexican children leave their shoes, along with water for the wise men's camels, by their doors to be filled with gifts.

◆ During the days before Christmas Eve, Mexicans have a procession called *Las Posadas* (las po•SA•das) where children dressed as Mary and Joseph sing and carry candles from house to house to find a place to rest. When they arrive at a designated house, they are invited in and have a Christmas party, complete with a piñata. The piñata, which the children must break with a stick while blindfolded, is full of toys and candy.

Literature Selections

◆ ***Nine Days To Christmas: A Story of Mexico*** by Marie Hall Ets and Aurora Labastida: Puffin, 1991. (Picture book, 48 pg.) This 1960's Caldecott Medal winner depicts a Christmas celebration in a Mexican town.

◆ ***The Legend of the Poinsettia*** by Tomie de Paola: G.P. Putnam's Sons, 1994. (Picture book, 32 pg.) This story tells of a girl who had nothing to give as a gift to the baby Jesus. She was told by a strange woman to give Jesus a bunch of weeds. People made fun of the girl when they saw her weeds, but because she gave the gift with love, the weeds magically turned into beautiful red flowers that started growing everywhere and spread around the land. The flowers were poinsettias.

Treat By Number

Many Mexican children play this game as a way to give gifts at Christmas. Each child chooses a slip of paper with a number written on it. The child matches the number on his slip to a prize with the same number. Write a number for each student on a small slip of paper. Divide the class into groups of four or five and let each child choose a slip. Have each group order get in numerical order. Combine the children into larger groups and have them continue ordering themselves. Eventually, have the entire class get in numerical order. Provide small treats or gifts labeled with numbers and let the children have the treats that match their numbers.

56

Ojos de Dios

Many Mexican children make Christmas ornaments, known as *Ojos de Dios* (O•hos de DEE•os) or God's eyes, from yarn. Give each child two craft sticks and several feet of yarn. Form a cross with the sticks and secure them by tying square knots using one end of a length of yarn. Beginning with the yarn behind the sticks, wind the yarn over and under the sticks as shown in the diagram. To change colors, hold the end of the first yarn and the beginning of the second yarn behind the sticks. Begin winding again, covering the ends. When the ornament is complete, cut the end and tuck it behind the woven pieces. Glue pom-poms to all ends and a loop of yarn to one end for hanging.

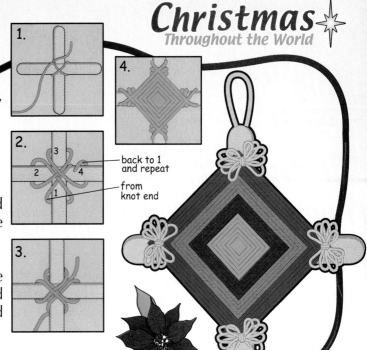

1.
2.
3.
4. back to 1 and repeat — from knot end

A Simple Gift

What colors are the flowers on a poinsettia? The answer is yellow, not red, pink, or white. This plant, which is native to Mexico, has green leaves, as well as colored leaves called *bracts*. The bracts are often mistaken for flowers, which are actually tiny yellow blooms in the center of each leaf cluster. Have students make poinsettia gifts to give loved ones. Cut brown paper grocery bags into terra cotta pot shapes. Glue a "pot" onto a large piece of dark blue construction paper. Color and cut out several poinsettia patterns (page 71) to glue above the pot. Create stems by twisting and gluing green paper from the pot to the flower. Glue yellow beads to the center of each bloom. Glue glitter stars in the background and attach a gift tag to the pot with a ribbon.

Mexican Nut Cookies

Help your class make these cookies enjoyed by people in Mexico throughout the Christmas season. The following recipe makes about four dozen cookies. Have children take turns beating the butter until creamy. Add sugar until the mixture is light and fluffy. Stir in the flour and nuts and mix well. Give each child a teaspoon of dough to shape into a 2-inch ball. Bake the cookies on greased baking sheets at 350° for 12-15 minutes. Remove cookies from the oven and let them cool slightly. Sprinkle the additional confectioner's sugar on a paper plate. While still warm, let the children roll their cookies in the sugar.

Ingredients
- 1 cup butter or margarine
- ¾ cup confectioner's sugar
- 2 cups sifted all purpose flour
- ¾ cup chopped nuts
- 5-6 tablespoons confectioner's sugar (for decoration)

Christmas in Germany

"Fröhliche Weihnachten"
(FRU•lih vi•NAWKT•ahn)

LITERATURE SELECTIONS

Christmas in Germany by Kristin Thoennes: Grolier Publications, 1999. (Reference book, 24 pg.) Tells about Christmas traditions in Germany.

The Cobweb Christmas by Shirley Climo: HarperTrophy, 1986. (Picture book, 32 pg.) An old woman cleans her house for Christmas and invites almost everyone in to see her tree.

DID YOU KNOW?

A traditional German Christmas begins long before December 25. Most Germans celebrate the Christmas season from St. Nicholas Day on December 6 to Epiphany on January 6.

Families make Advent calendars to count the days until Christmas. They also make Advent wreaths of pine branches with four candles. Each Sunday before Christmas, a candle is lit.

Many Germans bake traditional pastries during the season, including gingerbread and sweet bread called *stollen* (SHTO•len).

There are several gift givers in Germany. St. Nicholas puts gifts in children's shoes on the eve of December 6. Children also write Christmas wish lists to Christkindl (CHRIST•kint), or the Christ child, who looks like an angel. Weihnachtsman (vi•NAWKTS•man) is similar to Santa Claus, but he has a companion named Knech Ruprecht (knakt RUP•rakt) who gives switches to bad children.

"ADVENT"UROUS MATH

Ring in the season with this mathematical Advent calendar. On December 1, give each child a bell pattern (page 71). Assign each child a number from 1-24 to write on her pattern. Color the numbered side. Have students make up word problems, such as *How many days of school until Christmas?*, *How many meals will you eat before Christmas?*, *How many hours are left until Christmas?*, to write on the backs of their patterns. Staple the patterns, one at a time in numerical order, to a large sheet of poster board to make a calendar. Staple the pattern at the top to form a flap. Count down the days until Christmas, or winter break, by removing a pattern each day and having students solve the word problem.

December

Sunday	Monday	Tuesday	Wednesday	Thursday	Friday	Saturday
1	2	3	4	5	6	
8	9	10	11	12	13	
15	16	17	18	19	20	
22	23	24				

Christmas ✦
Throughout the World

ADVENT CENTERPIECE

The season will glow with these Advent wreath centerpieces. Have students cut five candle A patterns (page 71) and five candle B patterns (page 71) from construction paper; three purple, one pink, and one white. Top the candle B patterns with yellow paper flames. Cut the slits in the candles as indicated and fold over a short flap at the bottom of each candle A. Give each child a paper plate with the center cut out. Glue the candles to the plate, putting the white candle in the center. Crumple green tissue paper into balls. Glue the balls on the plate to fill out the wreath. Add berries made from red tissue paper. Children can "light" a candle on their centerpiece every Sunday by sliding a "lit" candle B onto a candle A.

 ## MINI TREE

The tradition of decorating a Christmas tree originated in Germany. Trees were decorated with candles, apples, and spice cookies called *lebkuchen* (leb•KOO•ken). Today, many parents secretly decorate the tree as a surprise for their children on Christmas Eve. Give each child a large pine cone to decorate as a "tree." If pine cones are not readily available in your area, they can be purchased at a craft store. Dot glue on the cones and sprinkle green glitter on the glue. When dry, glue on other decorations, such as beads or small candies. Wrap yellow yarn or metallic string around the trees for garlands. If desired, a star shaped piece of macaroni painted gold or a foil star can top the tree. Staple a strip of red construction paper into a small circle and place the tree inside to stabilize it.

GINGERBREAD COOKIES

Gingerbread can make sweet smelling Christmas ornaments, but it's more fun to eat! Make the recipe for gingerbread cookies in the *Make Your own Gingerbread* activity (page 23) the day before. Pack the cookies carefully in waxed paper. Give each child a cookie. Provide frosting, candies, sprinkles, and raisins. Let children decorate their cookies and enjoy them for a snack or give them as gifts.

Christkindl Bells

When Christkindl enters your house, tinkling bells can be heard, or so the legend goes. Let students make a Christkindl ornament with tinkling bells. Provide 8" x 8" pieces of white fabric, a pile of pine needles, and gold and yellow ribbon. Have each student crumble the pine needles and place them in the middle of the fabric. Gather all four corners and tie the ribbon around the fabric so the needles are in a bundle. Leave the two ribbon tails fairly long. The pine sachet will be the head of the Christkindl and the remaining fabric will be his gown. To create wings, bend a gold pipe cleaner into a figure 8 and glue plastic wrap to the back. Trim the excess plastic wrap from the edges. For hair, glue yellow yarn to the Christkindl's head. Bend a small section of gold pipe cleaner into a circle and glue it to the head as a halo or crown. Paint on a face and tie two small bells to the ribbon tails. Attach an ornament hook to the top of the head for hanging.

59

© Carson-Dellosa CD-2093

CHRISTMAS IN FRANCE
"JOYEUX NOËL"
(jhwah no•EL)

Did You Know?

- ⚜ Like most European countries, France celebrates the Christmas season for a month, from St. Nicholas Day on December 6 to Epiphany on January 6.
- ⚜ Preparations for Christmas include displaying the nativity scene, or *crèche* (cresh), complete with traditional handmade figures called *santons* (SAN tons).
- ⚜ Children put their shoes by the fireplace waiting for Père (pahr) Noël to fill them with gifts and treats. Père Noël travels with a partner, Père Fouettard (FWE tar), who reminds Père Noël of which children have not been good that year.
- ⚜ Families decorate their trees with foil stars, fruit, lights, and pine cones.
- ⚜ It is tradition to attend midnight services on Christmas Eve and then come home to a feast called *Le Réveillon* (le RE•ve•yon). Le Réveillon includes goose or turkey, oysters, sausages and ends with a cake shaped like a Yule log, called *bûche de Noël* (boosh de no EL). Presents are opened after the meal.

Literature Selections

The Acrobat and the Angel by Mark Shannon: Putnam Publishing Group, 1999. (Picture book, 32 pg.) Old French Christmas story dating back to the Middle Ages.

Christmas in France by Kristin Thoennes: Capstone Press, 1999. (Reference book, 24 pg.) Tells about Christmas traditions in France.

Réveillon Menu

The traditional Christmas Eve meal, Le Réveillon, means "waking up" and includes many courses of food. Have students plan menus for a special holiday dinner. Encourage students to include foods from all levels of the food pyramid. Ask them to think of special names for their dinners and write paragraphs explaining why they chose those foods and names for their meals. Fold a piece of construction paper in half, write the name of the meal on the outside, the menu on the inside, and the explanation on the back. Decorate with crayons and markers. Stand the menus up for display on a table or bookshelf.

Le Réveillon

Bûche de Noël

It is a European tradition to burn logs during the Christmas season called Yule logs. It was thought to be good luck to keep an unburned piece to light the next year's log. In France the bûche de Noël cake has taken the place of the real Yule log. Have students create their own Yule log cakes. Provide snack-sized cake rolls, chocolate frosting, and tubes of green, white, and red frosting. Frost the cake rolls to look like logs with bark, leaves, and flowers, then enjoy!

Community Santons

The making of santons, or nativity scene figures, is an honored tradition in France. Often, in addition to the Christmas story figures, community helpers, such as mayor, fisherman, police officer, etc., are made to place around the manger scene. Brainstorm a list of community helpers and let each child pick one to make into a santon. Mix together 1½ cups of salt, 4 cups of flour, and 1½ cups of water, and knead to form a dough. Give a small amount to each child and have her sculpt a figure of a person. Let the dough dry completely. Paint the figures like the chosen community helper. Display the completed figures in a scene with a sign reading *Our Community Santons*.

Hearth and Classroom

Deck the hearth with baskets of fruit, fa-la-la…It is tradition in France to keep a basket of fruit by the hearth at Christmas. Let students make 3-dimensional baskets of fruit to place by the *Fanciful Fireplace* (page 52). Cut out magazine pictures of fruit or draw fruit and cut out. Glue the fruit on a sheet of construction paper. Provide brown paper grocery bags and cut into ten-twelve 6" x 4" sections. Twist the sections into strips. Glue the twisted strips over the fruit in a criss-cross woven pattern. Leave some of the fruit uncovered so it appears to be piled up inside the basket. Twist a long piece of the bag into a handle. Display along the edges of the *Fanciful Fireplace* (page 52).

Père Noël Treat Toss

Père Noël fills French children's shoes with gifts and treats at Christmas. Give each child a small treat bag, containing a few candies wrapped in holiday paper and tied with a bow. Have each student take off one shoe, lay it on the ground, take six big steps back, and try to toss the treat bag into the shoe. If it goes in, that student get to eat her treats. After a few minutes, let each child take a step forward and try again. Let the children keep taking steps forward until the bags land in the shoes.

61

Christmas in Italy
"Buon Natale" (bwon•nah•TAHL•e)

La Befana

Did You Know?

- Christmas festivities begin in Italy with *Novena* (no•VE•nah), which is nine days of special prayers before Christmas. During Novena, shepherds come down from the mountains to play bagpipes, announcing Christmas is near.

- On Christmas Eve, families come together for a special feast that usually includes eel and other types of fish.

- Children receive gifts on Christmas from a Santa Claus-like figure called *Babbo Natal* (BAH•bo•na•TAHL) but most gifts are brought to children on Epiphany by an old woman called *La Befana* (la be•FA•na). The legend says the three kings invited La Befana to come with them to give gifts to baby Jesus. She was too busy cleaning and refused. After they left, she felt badly and wanted to go. Now, every year she travels around trying to find the three kings and the baby. She leaves gifts for children hoping one of them is Jesus.

Literature Selections

The Legend of Old Befana by Tomie de Paola: Harcourt Brace, 1980. (Picture book, 32 pg.) Learn why an old woman who rides a broom brings gifts to children in Italy.

Merry Christmas, Strega Nona by Tomie de Paola: Harcourt Brace, 1991. (Picture book, 32 pg.) Strega Nona prepares for a traditional Italian Christmas.

My Ceppo

A *ceppo*, or small triangular ladder, is often found in Italian homes around Christmastime. Instead of a tree, the ceppo is decorated with candles, ornaments, small gifts, family treasures, and most importantly, a nativity scene, or *precepio* (pre•CHE•pe•o). Ask students to think of things that are important to them and their families. Have each student draw her own ceppo and the things she would place on the shelves. Mount the paper on cardboard and decorate with markers, glitter, etc. Ask older students to write a page about their items; why they chose them and why they are important. Display the ceppos standing up on a table by gluing strips of cardboard to the backs as kickstands.

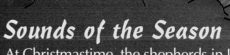

Hidden Letter

During the Christmas feast, Italian children often hide a letter in their father's napkin or under his plate promising to be good in the new year. Help students make the perfect present for a parent…a promise to be good! Have students write letters to their parents, explaining the ways they will be good in the year to come. Include promises of good behavior at school and at home. Write each letter on square paper and fold it in half diagonally to form a triangle. Turn the triangle so the long side is on the bottom and fold left and right corners to the outside, making the paper look like a napkin. Students can hide the letters underneath a parent's plate at dinner.

Sounds of the Season

At Christmastime, the shepherds in Italy come down from the mountains into the towns and play bagpipe music. Introduce students to the unique sounds of the bagpipe by inviting a bagpipe player to visit the class. Have the bagpipe player talk to students about how the instrument is played, some history of the instrument, and in what countries bagpipes are played. Then, ask the player to play some songs for the class.

Quick Quilling

Quilling is the traditional Italian art of curling strips of paper and gluing them together to form lacy designs. Many Italians create beautiful quilled ornaments to decorate their ceppos. Give each student several strips of white paper, about ¼″ wide. (Use thicker strips for younger students.) Roll the strips of paper into curls and glue them together in fancy designs. Show students how hearts, teardrops, and other designs can be made by rolling the paper from both ends and pinching folds in the curls. Create unique snowflake ornaments from the designs. Tie a ribbon to the top. Display with the *Christmas Throughout the World* bulletin board idea (page 16).

Be Befana

Let students pretend to be La Befana and search for the three kings. Before students arrive at school, hide three king patterns (page 72) glued to cardboard around the room, along with other pictures. Write messages on the other pictures with statements like, *The kings were here, but they just left* or *No one home…we've gone to see the baby.* Choose one child and give her a broom. Give her 15 seconds to find a king. Have her pass the broom to the next child and give him 15 seconds, and so on. If the three kings are found before every child gets to play, let the children who found the kings hide them for the next game.

Christmas in England

"Merry Christmas"

Did You Know?

* In England, Christmas trees are decorated with candles, cornucopias, and fruits. Stockings are hung by the fireplace. Letters written to Father Christmas asking for gifts are thrown into the fireplace rather than mailed. If the letters are drawn up the chimney by a draft, then the wishes will come true. If the letters are burned in the fire, another try is made.

* Father Christmas delivers presents to English children, which are opened on Christmas afternoon.

* The tradition of sending Christmas cards began in England. The cards were originally made on paper decorated by school children so that parents could see their children's progress in composition and penmanship. In 1843, an English artist, John Calcott Horsley, created the first Christmas card that people bought and sent to one another.

* The traditional Christmas meal in England includes turkey or roast beef, mince pie, which is made with raisins and mincemeat, and plum pudding.

Literature Selections

The Twelve Days of Christmas by Jan Brett: Dodd Mead, 1989. (Picture book, 32 pg.) The detailed artwork compliments the rhythmic reading of this classic English carol.

The Friendly Beasts: An Old English Christmas Carol by Tomie de Paola: Paper Star, 1998. (Picture book, 32 pg.) A traditional carol brought to life with sweet illustrations.

Peek-In Cards

Let students create Christmas cards in honor of this tradition. Have each child fold a half-sheet of watercolor paper like a card. Lightly sketch a Christmas scene on the inside. Paint the picture using watercolor paints. When dry, cut out four window pane panels on the front flap. Cover the panels with plastic wrap or laminating scraps, securing with clear tape. Paint frost in the corners of the window panes. A portion of the watercolor scene should show through the window. Have children write Christmas greetings to parents inside the cards in their best handwriting.

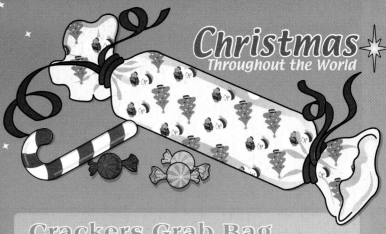

Puzzling Cards

Recycle those old Christmas cards and make fun and easy puzzles! Provide old Christmas cards or ask children to bring cards from home. Let students cut off the backs, keeping the pictures on the fronts. Cut the pictures into several pieces to create jigsaw puzzles. Puzzles can be made more durable if they are glued to poster board first. Let students switch puzzles and solve. Keep the puzzles in resealable bags so they can be used throughout the holiday season.

Holiday Greetings

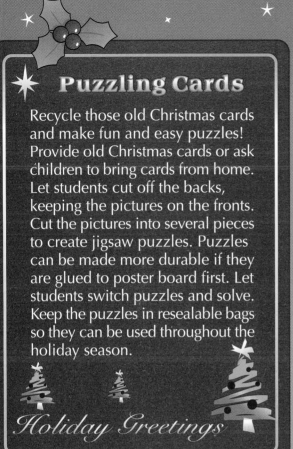

Crackers Grab Bag

Christmas crackers are popular in England. They were invented by Tom Smith, who, while watching his crackling fire one day, decided it would be nice if his presents could be revealed with a "crack" when opened. These "crackers" won't crack, but are fun to make. Ask parents to send in small treats or toys, sized to fit inside a short cardboard tube. Let students sponge paint tissue paper or use wrapping paper and cut into 12" x 8" pieces. Place the small gift (without showing students what it is!) inside the tube and wrap with the paper. Twist and tie the ends with ribbon and glue on glitter and sequins. Place the crackers in a large, decorated box. Let students pick one gift, making sure not to pick their own. All at the same time, crack open the crackers, revealing the gifts.

Wassail

English tradition also includes caroling from house to house on Christmas Eve. Tradition states that carolers would stop in for a drink from the *wassail* (WA•sal) bowl. Wassail is a hot punch and is often drunk with a toast for the new year. The word wassail comes from the old English *Was haile*, which was a wish for good health.

Ingredients:
cranberry juice
apple juice
cinnamon

Combine equal parts of the cranberry juice and the apple juice. Heat slightly in a microwave. Sprinkle cinnamon on top and serve in plastic foam cups, specially decorated by students. Let each child toast the holiday season as she enjoys her wassail.

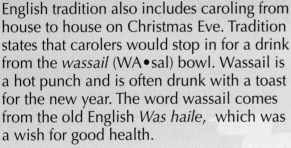

65

CHRISTMAS IN AUSTRALIA
"Merry Christmas"

Did You Know?

- Because Australia is located in the Southern Hemisphere, Christmas comes during the summer.

- The Christmas meal is often a picnic at the beach, complete with cold turkey, ham, salad, and plum pudding. Sometimes a coin or small gift is baked into the plum pudding which means good luck for whoever finds it.

- Australians decorate their homes with local greenery and flowers. The Christmas bush and Christmas bell are two favorites that flower during the holidays.

- Children hang stockings in their houses and wait for Santa Claus, and in some places, instead of arriving on a sleigh, he arrives by boat or surfboard!

- A very important tradition in Australia is the "Carols by Candlelight" concert. People from all over the country gather in the city of Melbourne on Christmas Eve to sing carols under the night sky.

Summer Santa

Create a change in latitude by having students imagine what a summer Santa would look like. In Australia, Santa probably does not wear a red wool suit trimmed with fur. Make a class list of comparable summer clothing and transportation for Santa (sleigh=boat, boots=sandals, etc.). Draw pictures and write descriptions of the summer Santas. Display on a bulletin board titled *Santa Down Under*.

Literature Selections

Christmas in Australia World Book Staff: World Book Inc., 1999. (Reference book, 80 pg.) Tells about Christmas traditions in Australia.

Christmas Cricket

Get into a summer state of mind by playing a simplified version of cricket with your students. Play this game in your gym or multipurpose room. Set up a Christmas tree (green cone or tube to represent a tree) with a small ball balanced on top (to represent a star). Divide the class into two teams. One student from the first team should stand in front of the cone with a bat or stick. Have one student from the other team stand 20-30 feet away with a large ball, such as a kickball. Have the second student roll the kickball at the cone and try to knock the ball off the Christmas cone. The student in front of the cone should try to deflect the ball with her stick. If the student rolling the ball knocks the ball off the cone, he earns a point for his team. If the other student keeps the ball from falling off the cone, she earns a point for her team.

66

Beautiful Bellflower

Australians often decorate at Christmas with a native flower called the bellflower. It is white and shaped like a bell with a yellow fringed edge. Give each student a small white paper cup. Poke a hole in the bottom and thread green yarn through the hole, securing it with a knot. Cut a strip of yellow tissue paper, glue it around the bottom of the cup, and cut fringes in it. Cut leaves from shiny green wrapping paper or construction paper and glue them to the top of the cup. Make a loop with the yarn and hang the bellflowers around the classroom.

Lucky Plum Pudding

Buy plum pudding to share with the class. Slip a gold foil-covered chocolate coin into the pudding as the lucky favor. Let each child have a serving of pudding and eat picnic-style on the floor. See who finds the lucky coin!

Carols by Flashlight

The "Carols by Candlelight" celebration in Melbourne is a popular tradition in Australia. Help students make their own candles and sing carols. Give each child a 10" x 6" piece of colored construction paper and decorate the front and back. Then, follow the steps below to complete the project.

Candle Base:

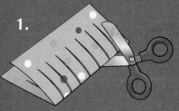
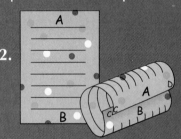

1. Fold the construction paper in half and cut as indicated, leaving a 1½" margin from the ends uncut.

2. Open the paper and roll it into a cylinder by overlapping the ends (A and B).

3. Tape the ends C and D together.

Candle:

1. Decorate a 7" x 9" piece of construction paper and roll into a cylinder. Tape the ends together.

2. Cut out the candle flame and candle glow patterns (page 72) from yellow and orange paper. Glue gold glitter on the ring and flame. Glue the flame to the inside edge of the ring.

3. Cut two 1" slits on opposite sides of the top of the candle tube and slide the glow ring and flame into the slits. Place the candle inside the candle holder.

When the candles are complete, turn out the lights and let students hold their candles and sing carols. Shine a flashlight on the candles and watch them sparkle.

Name _____

Solve the secret code to find out the names of each country's gift giver.

England

U.S. & Australia

France

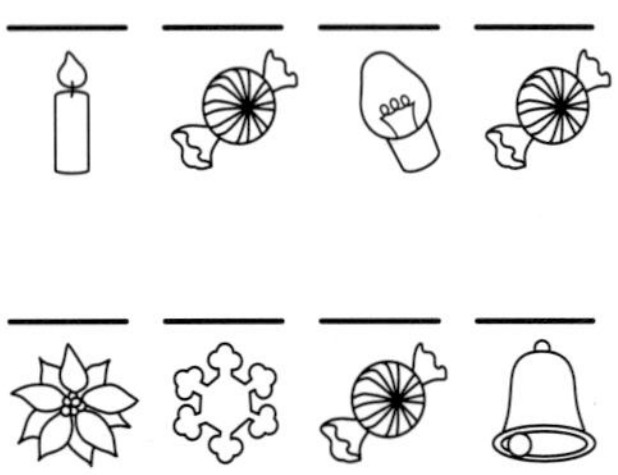

Germany

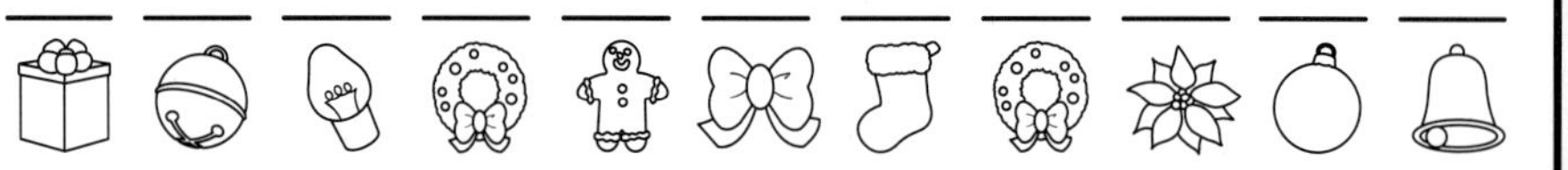

Italy

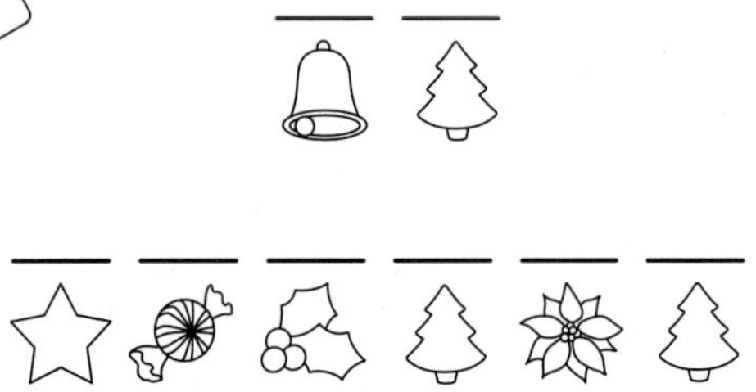

Mexico

KEY

A	B	C	D	E	F	G	H	I	J	K	L	M
N	O	P	Q	R	S	T	U	V	W	X	Y	Z

On a separate sheet of paper, write a descriptive paragraph about your tree.

Name _____

69

fireplace logs

stocking

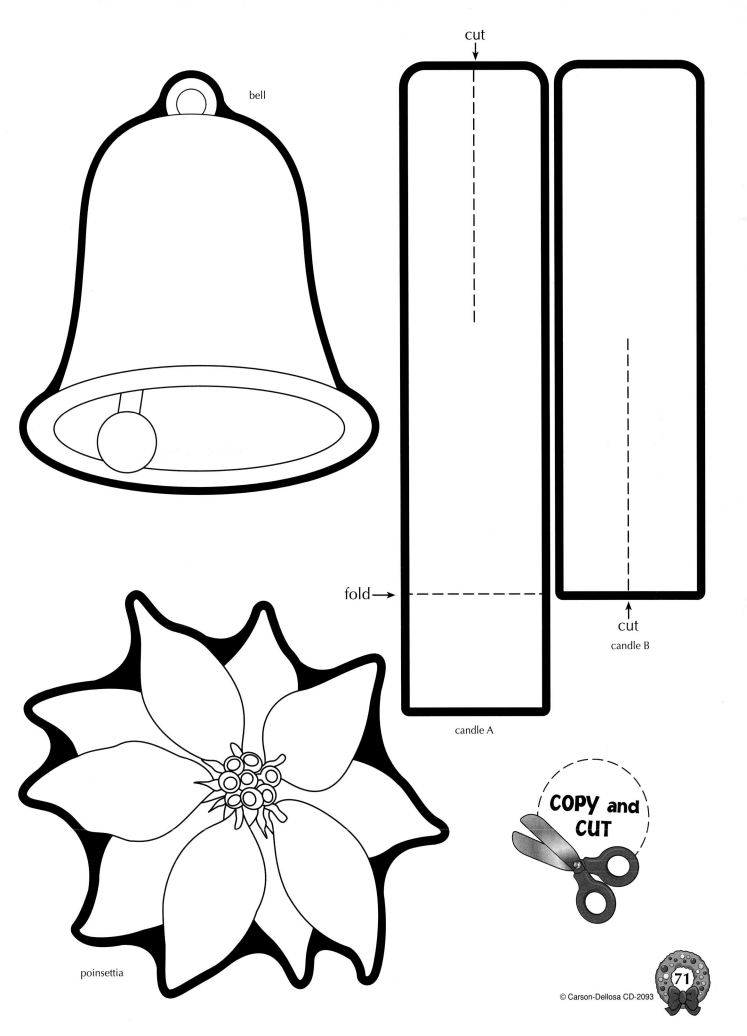

bell

cut

fold →

candle A

cut

candle B

poinsettia

COPY and CUT

candle flame

king

COPY and CUT

candle glow

Christmas tree

72

© Carson-Dellosa CD-2093

Gift-Giving Economics

Help children understand that the holidays are not just about getting gifts and cards, but also about giving to others and thinking of others.

Literature Selections

Alexander, Who Used to Be Rich Last Sunday by Judith Viorst: Atheneum, 1978. (Picture book, 32 pg.) Alexander decides how to spend the money his grandparents gave him.

Max Malone Makes a Million by Charlotte Herman: Henry Holt, 1992. (Picture book, 80 pg.) Max and his friend are always trying to strike it rich, but their neighbor is the one who succeeds.

Wants and Needs Collage

Encourage students to think about wants and needs before choosing that perfect gift. Create a list of needs, including water, food, air, clothing, and shelter. Then, have students make lists of wants. Ask what would happen if all wants were received but no needs. What might happen if all needs were received but no wants? Have students cut pictures of needs and wants from magazines to create collages. Challenge students to show in their collages the things they think are most important. Display the collages as one large collage on a bulletin board titled *Meeting Our Wants and Needs*.

Advertising Talk

Teaching students to understand advertising techniques can help them make better decisions about the quality of a product they would like to buy for a gift, rather than the quality of the advertising. Explain the following advertising techniques to students:

Celebrity Endorsement: A famous person or character is used to influence others to buy a product. Everyone else is buying this product, so why don't you?

Glamour: These ads rely on attractive models, lush scenery, and glitzy music to persuade consumers to buy.

Four out of Five: Four out of five professionals prefer this product.

We're #1: This implies that this product is the best.

Animation: These ads show the product doing unrealistic actions, such as running, talking, flying, etc.

Have students look through magazines and newspapers to find examples of these techniques. Let students share the ads they find with the class and tell which technique is used. If desired, ask students to listen or watch for these techniques in radio and television ads. Then, have them share which products they think would make high-quality gifts and why.

73

The Giving Circle

You are polite.

I have fun with you.

Gifts you cannot see are sometimes the best gifts of all. Cut a hole in a gift wrapped box. Put students' names in the box and have them sit in a circle. In the center, put the wrapped box. Have one student pick a name out of the gift box. As she passes the gift to the person she picked, she should say something nice to him, such as "You are helpful." He picks another name and passes the gift with a compliment, and so on, until every child has had a turn. Discuss how it felt to give and receive verbal gifts. Record all the verbal gifts on chart paper or sentence strips to display on a bulletin board with the title *Our Giving Circle*.

You are nice.

You are helpful.

I'm glad you are my friend.

You have good manners.

I trust you.

You are special.

Thrifty Wish List

The sky is not always the limit at the holidays. Let students create lists of gifts to buy for family members by cutting out magazine and catalog pictures, including prices, and gluing them onto long strips of paper. Then, have children prioritize their lists by giving them an imaginary $50 to spend. Let each child narrow down his list to the things he could buy. Have him write his choices on an index card, along with a math problem showing that the items total $50 or less. Display on a bulletin board titled *Our Thrifty Wish Lists*. As an extension, have students create a budget for gifts they would like to receive.

Homemade gifts are economical and easy to make! Set up these holiday centers, **"Egg"-ceptional Boxes** and **Perfect Pin-ups**, around your room to help students make inexpensive homemade gifts for family and friends. Then, wrap them in style with decorated paper grocery bags.

"Egg"-ceptional Boxes

Students can help adults get organized with these boxes. Place clean half dozen cardboard egg cartons at a center along with paint, buttons, sequins, ric-rac, and ribbons. Let each student paint an egg carton inside and out and decorate it. Punch holes in the lid at the front, thread ribbon through the holes, and tie a bow. Jewelry, coins, washers, nuts, bolts, etc., may be stored in these colorful boxes.

Perfect Pin-ups

Siblings or friends can display special pictures or notes and reminders on these handy gifts. Provide 7" x 9" pieces of foam core, 9" x 11" poster board frames with a 5" x 7" hole cut out, markers, fabric scraps, glue, buttons, beads, and small plastic trinkets. Let each student color her board with markers or glue on fabric. Color a frame and glue it to the board. Finish by gluing decorative items on the frame and a magnetic strip on the back for hanging.

PLACE PHOTO HERE

WINTER PLANTS

Long after other trees and plants have lost their leaves, evergreens are still fresh and fragrant. No wonder pine trees, holly boughs, and mistletoe are often displayed as winter decorations! Teach students about these unique trees and plants using these activities.

Did You Know?

Long ago, people believed evergreen trees lived forever since they did not seem to die or fade, even in the coldest winter weather.

Holly was once known as *holy tree* because it was used to decorate churches at Christmas.

Mistletoe was once used as a symbol of peace and hope. If two enemies met under a sprig of mistletoe, they would hug each other in friendship.

Literature Selections

How Nature Works by David Burnie: Reader's Digest, 1991. (Reference book, 192 pg.) Helpful resource containing information and hands-on experiments about evergreen trees and how they grow and survive.

Discover the Seasons by Diane Iverson: Dawn Publications, 1996. (Picture book, 48 pg.) Poems and colorful illustrations accompany each season, along with seasonal recipes and crafts.

More Than Christmas Trees

Evergreens, also known as *conifers*, are not just famous because they are decorated as Christmas trees. These trees are called evergreens because they do not lose their leaves all at once each year like deciduous trees. Instead, they shed their leaves, which look like needles, a few at a time, so they always have green leaves. To make a classroom evergreen tree, place a large sheet of white butcher paper on a covered work area. Provide bunches of evergreen needles and green paint. Use the needles as brushes to paint the paper. When the paint is dry, cut out a tree shape using an enlarged evergreen tree pattern (page 77). For the trunk, place a piece of butcher paper against a tree and rub over the surface with the side of a brown crayon, then add the trunk to the tree. To decorate the tree as shown, complete the *All About Evergreens* activity (page 76).

Conifers keep their leaves for up to four years.

All About Evergreens

Plant some evergreen knowledge with this activity! Have children research facts about conifers and write the facts on pine cone patterns (page 77) copied on brown paper. Display the facts on the tree from *More Than Christmas Trees* (page 75).

- Conifers keep their leaves for up to four years.
- Conifer seeds are protected by cones, not fruit.
- Cones open so seeds can be dispersed.
- Conifers have leaves that are long and slender (like sewing needles) or flat and scalelike.
- The pine scent given off by evergreens keeps insects away.
- Tough leaves protect conifer trees from cold weather and high winds.
- Conifers have flexible branches that bend, allowing heavy snow and ice to slide off without breaking the branches.

How Old Are You?

Say "Happy Birthday" to evergreens! Explain that pine trees, or evergreens, grow one cluster of branches each year. To tell the age of an untrimmed tree, count all of the branch clusters from the bottom to the top. Since pine seedlings do not have side branches for the first three years of growth, add three to the number. Locate pine trees outside and have students figure out their ages. If you live in an area where pine trees are not easily found, provide pictures of pine trees from nature magazines.

Deck The Halls With Mistletoe

These student-made mistletoe decorations will be just right for holiday decorating. To make a mistletoe decoration, have children paint their thumbs green and press them on white paper, making prints that resemble mistletoe leaves. Cut out the leaves and glue to a craft stick. Use pieces of crumpled white tissue paper for mistletoe berries. Display the decorations around a holiday bulletin board as a frame, or add them to the *Giant Holly Wreath* (at right).

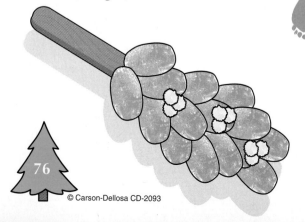

Giant Holly Wreath

Winter is the time for holly! Make a giant class holly wreath to display during the holidays. Place old newspapers on a large area of the classroom floor. Put several containers of green tempera paint at the top of a large piece of white butcher paper and a container of water and old towels at the bottom. Have students take off their shoes and socks, step in the paint, and create footprints in a circle shape to make a wreath. Then, have students step in the water to wash off the paint. If desired, have students trace their feet on green construction paper and cut them out instead. When the paint is dry, glue on crumpled red tissue paper balls for holly berries. Display the completed wreath on a door, wall, or bulletin board.

COPY and CUT

pine cone

evergreen tree

77

KWANZAA

Kwanzaa (KWAHN-zaah), a non-religious holiday that occurs each year from December 26 until January 1, is honored by many African-Americans. It lasts for seven days, with each day focusing on a different principle. Kwanzaa, which means *first fruits* in the Kiswahili language, was created in 1966 by Maulana Karenga as a way for people to celebrate African traditions and culture. The customs and symbols of Kwanzaa originate from African harvest festivals. Use this chapter to familiarize students with the principles and customs of this holiday.

LITERATURE SELECTIONS

Seven Candles for Kwanzaa by Andrea Davis Pinkney: Dial Book for Young Readers, 1993. (Picture book, 32 pg.) Introduces children to the history, symbols, and meaning of the Kwanzaa celebration.

Celebrating Kwanzaa by Diane Hoyt-Goldsmith: Holiday House, 1993. (Picture book, 32 pg.) Depicts how a family from Chicago plans for and celebrates Kwanzaa.

It's Kwanzaa Time! by Linda Goss: Putnam Publishing Group, 1995. (Reference book, 80 pg.) Artwork, songs, and recipes are presented in conjunction with the seven principles of Kwanzaa.

The Gifts of Kwanzaa by Synthia Saint James: Albert Whitman & Co., 1997. (Picture book, 32 pg.) Explains the origins of Kwanzaa as well as the seven principles associated with the holiday.

Kwanzaa by A.P. Porter: First Avenue Editions, 1991. (Reference book, 56 pg.) The traditions of Kwanzaa are presented in an easy-reader format.

HABARI GANI?

Each day of Kwanzaa begins with people asking *Habari gani?* (ha•BAH•ree GAH•nee) which means "What is the news of the day?" The family talks about the Kwanzaa principle of the day and what it means to them. On sheets of paper, let children draw pictures illustrating a Kwanzaa celebration. Below each picture, have the children write about what Kwanzaa means to them. To make a Kwanzaa book cover, let each child write "Habari gani?" across the top of a sheet of construction paper, then paint designs on the paper. Show pictures of African symbols and fabrics for them to use in creating the designs. Keep the Kwanzaa books in a center with other Kwanzaa-related objects.

LIGHT THE KINARA

The *kinara* (kee•NAH•rah) is a wooden candle holder with seven candles—three red (symbolizing the struggles Africans and African-Americans have faced), three green (representing a prosperous future), and one black (representing unity). On the first night of Kwanzaa, the black candle, which is in the center, is lit. On the remaining days, the black candle is lit again along with an alternating green (right side) or red candle (left side) until all of the candles are aglow on the last day. Let each child color and cut out a kinara pattern (page 87). Glue it to a sheet of construction paper. Trace and cut out a flame above each candle (adult help may be needed). Glue a sheet of orange construction paper behind the yellow sheet, leaving a 3" strip at the top unglued on either side. Cut two strips of yellow paper, each about 6¹/₂" long and 2¹/₂" wide. Slide a strip into each of the openings beside the candles. Pull the end of each strip to "light" the candles by exposing the orange flame underneath.

WEAVE A MKEKA

During Kwanzaa, a table is set with a colorful woven mat or *mkeka* (mm-KEE-kah). Tradition-ally, these mats are woven out of grasses or strips of fabric. Give each child one black and one white piece of construction paper. Fold the black paper in half and cut wavy or curved slits from the folded end to about 1" from the edge. Use markers to create bold designs on the white paper. Cut the paper into strips. Start the first row by weaving a white strip over the black paper, under the black paper, over, under, etc., continuing to the edge. For the next strip, begin by weaving under, then over, etc., and continue until all strips are woven. Weave three or four strands of natural raffia into the mat to resemble dry grasses.

MUHINDI DECORATIONS

Muhindi (moo-HIN-dee) are ears of corn placed on the table to represent the number of children in the family. If there are no children in the family, one ear of corn is placed on the table to show that children are important to everyone. Since the ears are the fruits of the cornstalk, they also represent the dreams and hopes parents have for future genera-tions. Tape plastic wrap to an arts and crafts table. Give each child several 2" x 2" yellow, orange, and brown tissue paper squares. Use a marker to draw a simple outline of an ear of corn on the plastic wrap. Fill the inside of the outline with a thin layer of glue and cover the outline with tissue paper squares. When the glue has dried, remove the "corn" from the plastic wrap and trim the edges into the shape of an ear of corn. Cut strips of paper from brown grocery bags and glue these to the top to resemble corn husks. Place these deco-rations on the mkekas, or use as window decorations.

79

KIKOMBE CHA UMOJA

Kwanzaa ends with a feast called a *karamu* (kah•RAH•moo). At the karamu, everyone takes a sip from the *kikombe cha umoja* (kee•KOM•beh cha oo•MOH•jah), or unity cup, to symbolize to-getherness. Let children make their own kiko-mbe cha umojas. Pro-vide plastic cups and have children paint them red, black, and green with acrylic paint.

SET A KWANZAA TABLE

This is one table children will love to set! Give each child a copy of the mkeka, kinara, muhindi, and kikombe cha umoja patterns (pages 86-87) to color and cut out. Glue the mkeka on a large sheet of construction paper, then add the kinara, muhindi, and kikombe cha umoja. Write *Kwanzaa yenu iwe na heri!* (KWAHN•zah YEH•noo EE•weh nah HEH•ree) (May your Kwanzaa be happy!). Finished projects can be displayed on a Kwanzaa bulletin board or classroom wall.

Kwanzaa yenu iwe na heri!

A PLENTIFUL HARVEST

Kwanzaa customs originated from African harvest festivals in which people gave thanks for plentiful crops. Fruits and vegetables, such as apples, bananas, pears, and yams, which represent the earth's plentiful crops or *mazao* (mah•ZAH•oo), are placed on the Kwanzaa table to acknowledge the harvest. Have each child make a fruit bowl to display on a Kwanzaa table. Fold a piece of construction paper in half and draw or glue pictures of fruits and vegetables on the paper. Cut out a wide bowl shape from brown construction paper. Glue some of the pictures to the top inside edge of the bowl. Fold the bowl in half so it curves outward. Put a small amount of glue on each side of the bowl. Keeping the bowl curved, attach it to the paper to create a 3-dimensional pop-out effect.

MAKE A BENDERA

The Kwanzaa flag is called a *bendera* (behn•DEH•rah) and is red, black, and green. Sometimes a bendera is hung on a wall be-hind the Kwanzaa table. Give each child a piece of white construction paper and have him turn the paper horizontally. Draw lines to divide the paper in three equal, horizontal sections. Color the top section black, the middle red, and the bottom green. Create a pole by gluing a piece of black paper around a long cardboard tube. Glue one side of the bendera to the side of the tube. Students can display their flags on their desks.

TASTY KWANZAA RECIPES!

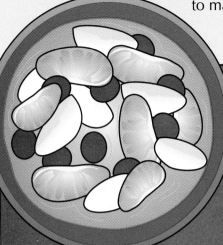

Below are some popular and tasty Kwanzaa dishes to make and share with the class.

HARVEST FRUIT SALAD

Fruit salad is often served as a way to give thanks for a plentiful harvest.

Ingredients:

3 oranges	$1^1/_2$ cups seedless grapes
3 pears	$1^1/_2$ cups orange juice
3 apples	

Peel and slice the oranges, pears, apples, and grapes. Place the fruit in a large bowl and mix with orange juice. Refrigerate until ready to serve. Makes about 10 servings.

BLACK-EYED PEA SALAD

Many people believe eating black-eyed peas on New Year's Eve will bring good luck in the upcoming year.

Ingredients:
2 16-ounce cans black-eyed peas, rinsed
1 medium onion, chopped
2 stalks of celery, chopped
1 red bell pepper, seeded and chopped
1 bottle basil vinaigrette salad dressing

Cook peas according to package directions. Let them cool completely. In a large bowl, combine the peas, chopped onion, celery, bell pepper, and salad dressing. Cover and refrigerate at least two hours before serving. Makes about 24 servings.

KWANZAA COOKIES

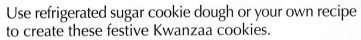

Use refrigerated sugar cookie dough or your own recipe to create these festive Kwanzaa cookies.

Ingredients:
Refrigerated sugar cookie dough
Wooden craft sticks
Red, green, and black frosting
Flour

Roll or press the dough on a floured surface to $^1/_8$" thickness. Use a plastic knife to cut dough into rectangles. Give each child two rectangles and have them sandwich a craft stick between the cookies to resemble a flagpole. Bake the cookies according to the package directions and cool. Decorate the cookies to look like Kwanzaa flags by using the frosting to create red, black, and green stripes on the cookies.

KWANZAA GIFTS

Zawadi (zah•WAH•dee) are gifts given during Kwanzaa that often reflect African culture.

APPLIQUÉ PICTURE

Some African tribes use appliqué designs as decorations. Appliqué is created by cutting out brightly colored shapes from cloth and sewing them to black fabric. Let each child cut out shapes from construction paper. Glue the shapes to black construction paper and use a fine-point pen to add stitching marks around the objects so they appear sewn. Punch holes in the top corners and tie a length of yarn to make a hanger.

BEADED JEWELRY

Beads have been made and traded in Africa for centuries. Many different materials, such as shells, seeds, stones, and glass, can be used to make beads. Have students make their own beads to create necklaces. Prepare a batch of self-hardening salt dough (see recipe at right). Let students mold small amounts into various shapes. Slide a drinking straw through the center of each bead, and let dry overnight. The next day, remove the beads from the straws allowing the inside to dry. When the beads have dried completely, paint them using tempera or acrylic paint. String the finished beads on a length of natural raffia, knotting the ends together to make a necklace to wear or give as a Kwanzaa gift.

SELF-HARDENING SALT DOUGH

Ingredients:
4 cups flour
1½ cups salt
1½ cups water

Mix salt and flour together in a large bowl. Add water gradually as you mix the ingredients with a spoon. Knead the dough, adding water if it is too crumbly or flour if it is too sticky. Dough will harden if left to air dry for several days or can be baked at 300° for 30-40 minutes.

HAPPY KWANZAA CARD

Children can make mosaic greeting cards to extend Kwanzaa wishes to friends and family. Give each child a piece of black construction paper to fold in half. Provide scraps of yellow, orange, green, and red construction paper to cut into small shapes. Glue the shapes to the paper, leaving some black space between them to create a design. Let children write Kwanzaa greetings and sign their names on the insides of the cards using a paint or glitter pen.

Happy Kwanzaa! from Kim

PRINCIPLES OF KWANZAA

THE NGUZO SABA

THE NGUZO SABA

UMOJA

KUJICHAGULIA

UJIMA

UJAMAA

NIA

KUUMBA

IMANI

The seven principles of Kwanzaa are known as *The Nguzo Saba* (nn•GOO•zoh SAH•bah). Many people display The Nguzo Saba during the holiday. Copy The Nguzo Saba pattern (page 88) for each student to color and cut out. Color the harvest fruits and vegetables on the pattern, or cut out and glue fruits and vegetables from magazines to create a border. Fold four pieces of paper in half and bind them to the pattern, making a book. On the appropriate day, have children write about what each principle of Kwanzaa means to them. On the last page, write and illustrate Kwanzaa greetings.

UMOJA

On the first day of Kwanzaa the principle *Umoja* (oo•MOO•jah), or unity, is the focus. Family and community are emphasized. Give each child a large sheet of construction paper and three or four blank index cards. On the index cards, have the children illustrate special things they have done with their families. Glue the cards to the construction paper. Under each picture, children can write sentences describing the event.

KUJICHAGULIA

The second day of Kwanzaa focuses on *Kujichagulia* (koo•jee•chah•goo•LEE•ah) or self-determination. Making your own decisions and shaping the future are focal points. Give each student a sheet of drawing paper. Have her draw a self-portrait showing what she wants to be when she grows up and write a paragraph telling how she plans to reach her goal. Post the portraits to give others a look into the future. Title the display *Shaping Our Future*.

83

YOU DECIDE

Help students understand the importance of being responsible and making their own decisions, an important aspect of Kujichagulia. Copy the *You Decide* worksheet (page 88). Divide the class into small groups and give each group a different scenario. Have students talk about what they would do in each situation and why. Each group member should share and explain his decisions to the others.

UJIMA

Ujima (oo•JEE•mah) (collective work and responsibility) is the focus of the third day of Kwanzaa. Help children realize how their families work together. Let the children trace their hands on red and green construction paper and cut out. Next, have students write the name of a family member at the bottom of each hand shape. On each finger, they can write something this person does to help the family. On a piece of black construction paper, glue the handprints with thumbs touching and write family names in the center. Students can take home the finished projects to share.

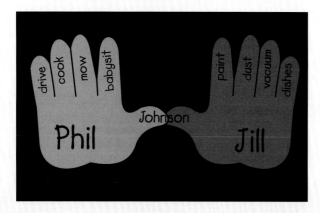

UJAMAA

The fourth day of Kwanzaa emphasizes *Ujamaa* (oo-jah-mah) or buying goods and services from neighborhood businesses to support and help communities grow. Some families save money to purchase a gift the family will enjoy. Have children make special banks to save for such a Kwanzaa gift. Ask each child to bring in an empty cardboard container with a lid (such as an oatmeal container). Cover the container by gluing a piece of black construction paper around it. Glue paper scraps and sequins, beads, etc., to the container to create a design. Cut a small slit in the lid and replace it on the container. Have the children take their banks home and encourage family members to save money for a family Kwanzaa gift.

NIA

5TH DAY

Purpose or *Nia* (NEE•ah) is the focus of the fifth day of Kwanzaa and emphasizes having a reason or purpose for everything you do. Using your skills and knowledge to make a difference for the future and setting goals to learn new skills is also part of Nia. Give each child a large sheet of white paper to fold in half. On one half, have her illustrate and write about skills and talents she has. On the other half, have her illustrate and write about skills she would like to learn. Challenge children to think of ways they can use their skills to make a difference in their communities, homes, or schools.

KUUMBA

6TH DAY

The sixth day of Kwanzaa focuses on *Kuumba* (koo•OOM•bah) or creativity. Expressing oneself through music, dance, art, and storytelling is featured. African rainsticks are traditionally made from gourds and seeds grown in Africa. Pins or nails are placed through the gourd and create a soothing sound similar to rain when the seeds inside strike against them. Children can make their own rainsticks using cardboard tubes, dry rice, and long pins. Push 30-40 pins through the tube. Distribute the pins evenly over the entire surface. Glue brown construction paper around the tube. Decorate and cover one end of the tube by securing several tissue paper squares around it with a rubber band. Pour 1/2 cup of dry rice into the tube. Cover and secure the other end. Gently turn the rainsticks up and down and listen to the sounds. Have volunteers create dances to accompany the rainstick music.

THE KWANZAA KARAMU

The sixth day of Kwanzaa includes a special feast called a *karamu* (kah•RAH•moo). Family and friends gather and bring food to share. Often the karamu coincides with the celebration of New Year's Eve, so foods that are thought to bring good luck, such as black-eyed peas and collard greens, are served. Dancing, storytelling, music, and speeches make up the karamu ceremony. Everyone drinks from the kikombe cha umoja to honor African-American ancestors. Plan a classroom karamu celebration. In addition to the recipes on page 81, encourage children to share experiences, stories, and songs about Kwanzaa.

IMANI

7TH DAY

Imani (ee•MAH•nee) (faith) is the focus of the seventh and last day of Kwanzaa. Having faith in yourself, your family, and leaders, and reflecting upon the efforts of others is emphasized. In some families, Imani includes hearing and writing stories about African-American ancestors who worked toward change. Provide books about African-American leaders, such as Martin Luther King, Jr., Harriet Tubman, and Sojourner Truth. Let each child choose a person and write a short biography. Cut and decorate strips of black, red, and green paper to frame the finished works. Display the biographies on a bulletin board.

85

mkeka

86

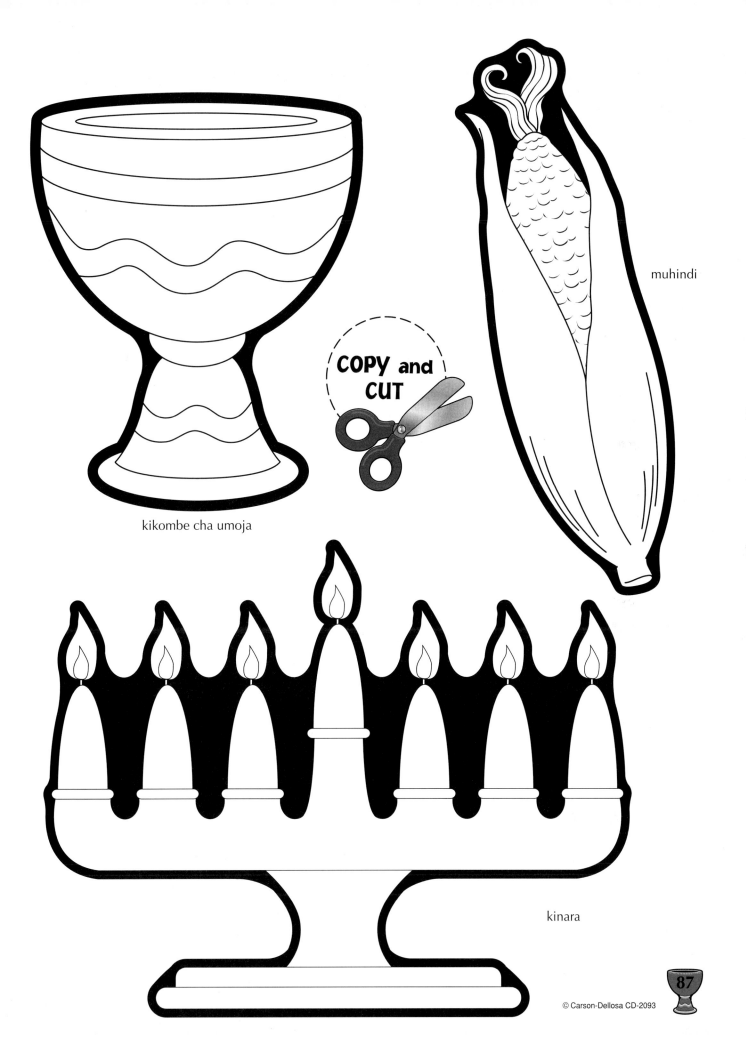

COPY and CUT

kikombe cha umoja

muhindi

kinara

You Decide

Your friends want you to go outside, not study.	You accidentally break your friend's new game.
The math problems you are working on are hard.	Your friends are buying candy, but you forgot your money.
One of your friends is making fun of another friend.	You are supposed to watch your brother, but you want to play with your friends.
You forgot to do your homework.	You want to buy a video game, but you do not have enough money saved.
Your teacher asks you to take a note to the office.	You want to play one game and your friend wants to play another game.

THE NGUZO SABA

UMOJA
KUJICHAGULIA
UJIMA
UJAMAA
NIA
KUUMBA
IMANI

The Nguzo Saba

A Wonderland of Winter Books

Winter is a great time to curl up with a good book! Share these wonderful stories and fun activities with your students!

Snowballs

by Lois Ehlert: Harcourt Brace & Company, 1995. (Picture book, 32 pg.)

When the first snowfall finally arrives, a snow family is made and decorated using "good stuff," such as popcorn, yarn, and buttons. The story describes each member of the snow family and what happens when the sun inevitably melts each one.

Several days before the project, set out a container in which children can save "good stuff" to use as decorations for snow people. Give each child one 11" x 17" piece of blue and several 8½" x 11" pieces of white construction paper. Create snow figures by tearing the white paper and gluing the shapes on the blue paper. Use objects from the class collection of "good stuff," as well as buttons, popcorn, wallpaper, fabric scraps, yarn, and sequins to add features and clothing to the snow people. Have children name their snow people. Display the finished projects on a wintry bulletin board display.

Chilly Billy

Snow

by Uri Shulevitz: Farrar Straus Giroux, 1998. (Picture book, 32 pg.) (**Caldecott Honor Book**)

A lone snowflake falls over a city, but no one thinks anything of it except a boy and his dog. As one snowflake turns into many snowflakes, the townspeople are surprised to see everything eventually blanketed by white snow.

Cover a bulletin board or wall section with blue paper. Let each child trace and cut out a large circle from white paper. Fold in half, then fold it again into thirds. Cut shapes into the folded edges and along the top without cutting the shape in half. When the paper is opened, a snowflake shape will appear. Have the children sit in a circle. As you read the story aloud, stop when the number of snowflakes falling is mentioned in the text. As you say the number, choose a matching number of students to tape their snowflakes to the blue paper. Continue reading and having students post snowflakes until each child has had a turn. Talk about how all of the students' snowflakes combined to create a huge snowfall, just like in the story!

89

The Jacket I Wear in the Snow

by Shirley Neitzel: Mulberry Books, 1994. (Picture book, 32 pg.)

Using rhyming text and rebus, the story tells of all the different pieces of clothing a little girl needs to put on before going outside to play in the snow. When the outdoor fun has ended, the story describes what happens to the wet clothes once back indoors.

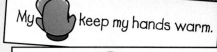
My [mittens] keep my hands warm.

I zip up my [jacket] all the way.

My [socks] got wet outside.

Point out to students how pictures are used in the sentences to tell the story. Have students cut out four pictures of wintertime clothing from magazines, then cut a piece of 11" x 17" paper into strips. Instruct students to write one sentence on a strip for each picture, then glue the picture to the strip in place of the word to create a rebus story. Students can trade stories with classmates and let them read and place the strips in the correct order.

Award Winners

The Polar Express

by Chris Van Allsburg: Houghton Mifflin Company, 1985. (Picture book, 32 pg.)
(Caldecott Medal Winner)

One Christmas Eve, a boy takes a magical journey to the North Pole on a train called The Polar Express. While there, he is selected to choose the first gift of Christmas. He chooses a silver bell from a reindeer harness, which is lost on his trip home. Surprisingly, he awakens Christmas morning to find a wrapped gift under the tree containing the special bell.

Engage children's imaginations by asking what they would have chosen as the first gift of Christmas. Provide construction paper and have each child draw a large toy sack and cut it out. Illustrate and write about the gift. Decorate the paper to look like Santa's toy sack, complete with cotton ball trim. Finish the project by attaching a tiny jingle bell to the top of the toy sack.

I would ask Santa if I could drive his sleigh and deliver toys around the world. Paul

The Snowy Day

by Ezra Jack Keats: Scholastic, Inc. 1962. (Picture book, 32 pg.)
(Caldecott Medal Winner)

Peter wakes up to see snow covering everything outside. He puts on his snowsuit and begins a day of snowy adventures such as building a snowman and sliding down a snow-covered hill.

Jodie's Snowy Day

Have each child cut out a stick-figured paper shape and glue it to construction paper. Let children cut out magazine pictures of hats, mittens, boots, scarves, and other winter clothing. Glue the pictures and draw details on the figure to make it look like a person. In the background, have students draw things they would do on a snowy day, like build a snowman, make a snow angel, draw tracks in the snow, etc. Let each child title his work _____'s *Snowy Day.*

Owl Moon

by Jane Yolen: Philomel Books, 1987. (Picture book, 32 pg.)
(Caldecott Medal Winner)

An excited little girl goes owling with her father late one winter night. They silently walk through the moonlit woods, looking and hoping to see an elusive owl. When they reach a forest clearing, her father calls out and suddenly a majestic owl appears!

Before the students arrive at school, cut simple forest animal silhouettes from black construction paper and hide them around the classroom. If desired, trace the animal patterns on pages 48-51. Post a large owl on a bulletin board, adding reflective tape or aluminum foil for eyes. After reading the story, darken the room and have children look for other animals hiding in the forest. Explain that along with owls, other animals are active at night. When an animal is spotted, turn the flashlight on the silhouette for everyone to see!

The Mitten

by Jan Brett: G.P. Putnam's Sons, 1989. (Picture book, 32 pg)

When a boy loses his white mitten, several forest animals snuggle inside it to keep warm. Suddenly a bear sneezes, sending the mitten—and the animals—flying into the air.

Give each child blue paper and crayons to draw a winter forest scene. Sponge paint the scene to make snow-covered trees and snowbanks. Draw and cut two mitten shapes from white paper. Use a pencil to add knitting details to one mitten, then draw forest animals on the other mitten. Glue the mitten with the drawn animals to the wintertime scene. Tape or glue the top of the plain mitten over the decorated mitten, leaving the sides unattached so the top mitten can be lifted to see the animals inside. Children can trade scenes with classmates and name the animals they see inside each mitten.

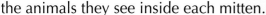

91

Snowflake Bentley

by Jacqueline Briggs Martin: Houghton Mifflin Company, 1998. (Picture book, #32 pg.) **(Caldecott Medal Winner)**

This book tells the true story of Wilson Bentley, a man who spent his life studying and photographing snowflakes. It describes the different techniques and methods he used to capture the beauty of snowflakes and the discoveries he made through his work.

After sharing the story, create permanent impressions of snowflakes by spraying a pane of glass with aerosol hair spray. (Chill the glass and hair spray in a refrigerator first.) Store the spray-covered glass in a freezer until ready to use. Take the glass outdoors and allow snowflakes to fall on it. Then, bring the glass indoors and allow it to dry for about 15 minutes. Although the snowflakes will melt, their impressions will be held by the hair spray, enabling the shapes and designs of the snowflakes to be examined with magnifying glasses. In a science journal, have children draw and describe the snowflakes.

The Snowman

by Raymond Briggs: Random House, Inc., 1978. (Picture book, 32 pg.)

This wordless picture book tells the story of a boy who builds a snowman that comes to life. He invites the snowman into his home and introduces him to many strange things, like lamps and television sets. In turn, the snowman takes the boy flying through the night sky to show him his wintry world.

After sharing the story, have each child illustrate and write an adventure story about a snowman who comes to life. Have students decide how many pictures they will use to illustrate their stories. Each student should number a piece of paper with the number of pictures she will draw and then write sentences describing what will be drawn. Then, divide a sheet of white paper into the appropriate number of spaces and illustrate the sentences. Paint each scene using watercolors. Let classmates "read" the stories using only the pictures.

92

INTERNATIONAL Holidays

St. Nicholas

St. Nicholas is similar to the United States' celebration of Christmas. Every year, on the night of December 5, many children in Slovakia and other parts of eastern Europe are visited by St. Nicholas, the patron saint of children. On the eve of St. Nicholas, children place polished boots on their windowsills and leave one window half open so that St. Nicholas may enter and leave toys and treats. For the good children, he leaves toys, candies, and chocolate treats. For the naughty children, he leaves coal, potatoes, and onions. Usually, children receive a combination of "good" and "naughty" gifts to show that they have been both good and bad.

Jolly Old St. Nicholas

Falling in love with St. Nick will happen quickly when students make these St. Nicholas faces! St. Nicholas looks a little bit like Santa Claus with his red coat, red pants, and white beard, but he also wears a bishop's hat. Provide each student with a piece of white construction paper, a piece of red construction paper, glue, cotton balls, crayons, and glitter. Have each student cut a face shape from the white construction paper and draw eyes, a nose, and a mouth on the shape. Next, have them cut a bishop's hat from the red construction paper and glue it to the top of the face. Students can create St. Nicholas's beard by gluing cotton balls to his face. As a final touch, allow students to glue glitter to the hat. Display the St. Nicholas faces on a wall or bulletin board.

Boot Up Some Fun!

Make these St. Nicholas boots in a few easy steps! Provide each student with a large white sock and two cardboard tubes. Have students decorate the socks with fabric markers, glitter glue, beads, yarn, etc. Next, ask students to place one cardboard tube in the foot of the sock and the other at the neck so that the sock remains open. Display the boots on a windowsill. Add small candy treats as a surprise for students when they come to class the next day.

93

St. Lucia

Lucia is the saint of light and every December 13, one of the longest and darkest winter nights in Sweden, she is celebrated. One girl is chosen to be Lucia, and wears a long white gown tied with a red sash. On her head she wears a crown of lingonberry and candles. Following her are other girls dressed in white carrying candles. Also tending to Lucia are starboys dressed in long white shirts and pointed caps decorated with silver stars. Usually, each school has its own St. Lucia procession. Children sing traditional songs and eat gingerbread cookies and saffron buns with raisins called *lussekatts* or Lucia cats.

Star Light and Candles Bright

Radiating enjoyment won't be hard for students when they make these St. Lucia crowns! First, have students decide if they want to make a St. Lucia or starboy crown. For St. Lucia Crowns: Cut 2" wide strips of green paper for each crown, long enough to fit around a child's head plus an additional 2". Glue or tape the ends together to form a headband. Then, provide students with yellow and orange construction paper. Have students cut 4" strips from the yellow paper, to resemble candles. Next, tell students to cut candle flames from the orange construction paper. Have students tape or glue the "candle flames" to the candles. Finally, ask students to glue or tape the candles to the crown. For starboys: Provide each student with a paper cone large enough to fit on his head. To make the cone, roll a large piece of construction paper into a cone shape and tape the ends. Next, supply star shapes cut from cardboard. Instruct students to wrap aluminum foil around two or three of the cardboard stars, then glue or tape the stars to the cones. Now, have a class St. Lucia procession by allowing students to parade around the room in their new crowns!

Gingerbread Treats

Make some tummies growl by decorating these gingerbread treats with the class! Gingerbread cookies are a traditional staple during St. Lucia in Sweden. Bring in a box of gingerbread cookies and different colors of frosting. (A few drops of food coloring in white frosting can be used for this step.) Place the frostings, craft sticks, and cookies at a craft center. Have students decorate the cookies with images that represent light. Students may wish to decorate cookies with frosting candles, lightbulbs, fireflies, etc. Once the cookies are decorated, allow students to admire their classmates' creations before indulging themselves with these yummy treats!

St. Lucia Buns

During St. Lucia, it is customary to eat buns. Make the following recipe to share with the class during your St. Lucia celebration.

St. Lucia Buns

5½ teaspoons active dry yeast
4 to 4½ cups all-purpose flour
¾ cup sugar
1 teaspoon salt
1 cup milk
⅛ teaspoon powdered saffron **or**
½ teaspoon saffron threads
½ cup (1 stick) butter, cut up
2 large eggs, slightly beaten

In a large mixing bowl, combine the yeast, 2 cups flour, sugar and salt. In a small saucepan, heat milk to simmering over medium heat, then remove from the heat. Add the saffron and butter; stir until the butter is melted and the mixture has cooled to very warm. Stir the liquids into the flour mixture and add eggs. Beat with a wooden spoon until the batter is smooth and satiny. Beat in the remaining flour one cup at a time until the dough is stiff but not dry. Cover and refrigerate for at least 2 hours. To bake, preheat oven to 400º. Form the dough into "S" shapes and bake for 8-10 minutes.

Glowing Candles

Have a traditional school St. Lucia celebration. Provide a piece of construction paper, a small square of poster board, and gold glitter for each student. Roll the construction paper into a tube and tape at both ends. Have students cut flame shapes from the poster board and glue on gold glitter. Cut a slit in the side of each candle to hold the flame. Let students hold the candles and sing carols, like the one below.

St. Lucia

(Sing to the tune of *Are You Sleeping?*)

O, Saint Lucia,
O, Saint Lucia,
Shining bright,
Wearing white,
Lighting up the darkest
Lighting up the darkest
Winter night,
Winter night.

Boxing Day

Though the origins of this holiday are still unknown, Boxing Day, December 26, is celebrated in Britain, Australia, New Zealand, and Canada and may date back as far as the Middle Ages. If Boxing Day falls on a Saturday or Sunday, then it is celebrated the following Monday. Traditionally, boxes filled with money, gifts, and food were given to the poor, people in service jobs (mail carrier, paper carrier, milk delivery person), and charities on December 26. Parents also gave small gifts to their children such as fruit or handkerchiefs. Today, many businesses still follow the original tradition of Boxing Day by donating food, time, money, or holiday gifts to those less fortunate. Families usually spend the day at home relaxing or at gatherings with friends.

Draw Out the Holidays

Sharing their holiday experiences will be easy for students when they draw their favorite memories! Place several watercolor paints, paintbrushes, and a few cups of water at a work station. Give each student a piece of 8½" x 11" heavy white paper and allow him to paint a picture of his favorite holiday memory. Once the pictures have dried provide students with a 12" piece of ribbon. Ask students to roll up their painted pictures and tie the ribbon around them. These pictures will be the gifts included in the next activity.

Boxes of Joy

Containing their excitement will be impossible for students when they make these holiday boxes! Provide a cereal box for each student along with wrapping paper, tissue paper, markers, stickers, beads, ribbon, etc. Have students decorate their boxes. If desired, ask students to write simple holiday messages to attach to the boxes. Next, have students place their holiday pictures from *Draw Out the Holidays* (above) inside the boxes. Take the boxes to a local nursing home or hospital to share with the patients who may see these gifts as boxes of joy!